Edmund Hatfield

The legend of St. Ursula and the virgin martyrs of Cologne

The Text Printed within Engraved Borders of Scenes in the Life of St. Ursula

Edmund Hatfield

The legend of St. Ursula and the virgin martyrs of Cologne
The Text Printed within Engraved Borders of Scenes in the Life of St. Ursula

ISBN/EAN: 9783744650960

Hergestellt in Europa, USA, Kanada, Australien, Japan

Cover: Foto ©ninafisch / pixelio.de

Weitere Bücher finden Sie auf **www.hansebooks.com**

THE LEGEND
OF
SAINT URSULA.

" It is with feelings of respect and love that we have for a long time studied the innumerable traditions of past generations, with whom Christian faith and Christian poesy, the grandest lessons of religion, and the most exquisite creations of the fancy were so intimately blended, that to separate them would be impossible. If we have not the happiness to receive with perfect simplicity the wonders of divine power which they relate, yet we have not the courage to despise the innocent traditions which have for so many ages charmed thousands of our brethren. Should any thing among them seem to savour of puerility it is exalted and sanctified in our eyes as being the faith of our fathers—of those who were nearer Christ than ourselves ; and we have not the heart to contemn that which they believed with so much fervour, and loved with such devotion."

MONTALEMBERT, *Histoire de Sainte Elisabeth*.

" The miracles of the middle ages have ever excited popular enthusiam. Many other narrations of the same kind are interesting and agreeable ; for one finds therein much which is not to be met with elsewhere—quickened emotions, and thoughts both elevated and tender ; the manifestation, in fine, of the people, who, at that period, unless they were within the bosom of the Church, were everywhere debased."

GUIZOT, *Histoire de l'église de Reims*.

THE LEGEND

OF

SAINT URSULA

AND THE

VIRGIN MARTYRS OF COLOGNE

The Text printed within Engraved Borders of Scenes in the
Life of St. Ursula.

London:
JOHN CAMDEN HOTTEN, PICCADILLY.
1869.

CONTENTS.

	PAGE
TITLE	i
CONTENTS	v
INTRODUCTION	ix

PART I.

THE LEGEND OF SAINT URSULA.

CHAPTER I.

PAGE

Parentage of Saint Ursula—Agrippinus, King of the Picts, and his son Conan—Embassy to the Court of Dionotus, father of Ursula, with proposals of Marriage   1

CHAPTER II.

The Ambassadors of Agrippinus arrive at the Court of Dionotus—Ursula is directed by a Vision—The answers of Dionotus to the Embassy—The Messengers return to Agrippinus . 9

CHAPTER III.

Building the Vessels for the Company of Virgins—Saint Ursula and Dionotus visit the Shipwrights—The Virgins assemble at the Court of Dionotus—The names of the principal Commanders—The Fleet exercises in the Harbour of Plymouth. 15

CHAPTER IV.

Departure of the Fleet from Britain—Arrival at Thiel, in Holland—Their Reception—The Fleet proceeds to Cologne—Welcome of the Archbishop and Sigillindis . 25

CHAPTER V.

The Vision of Saint Ursula at Cologne—She leads her companions to Rome—Their reception by Cyriacus, the Pope 33

CHAPTER VI.

The Departure from Rome—The Vision of Cyriacus—Arrival of the Company at Bâle—Conan prepares an expedition in search of Saint Ursula—He arrives at Mayence—Is instructed by Rutherius in the principles of Christianity—Saint Ursula and her Companions arrive at Mayence—Meeting of Saint Ursula and Conan—Conan is Baptised—The Martyrs leave Mayence   43

CHAPTER VII.

The Emperor Maximinus publishes an edict against the Christians—The Company of Virgins approach Cologne—The Exhortation of Cyriacus—The Fleet arrives at the City—The Huns fall upon the defenceless Martyrs—The Massacre miraculously stayed—Saint Ursula and Conan led before Aasvahs, the Barbarian Leader—The Execution of Conan—The proposal of Aasvahs to Saint Ursula—The Saint's temptation   55

CHAPTER VIII.

The noble resolution of Saint Ursula—Aasvahs gives orders for her Execution—She receives her Eternal Crown—Conclusion   63

CONTENTS.

PART II.

METRICAL LEGEND OF SAINT URSULA.

	PAGE
FACSIMILE OF WYNKYN DE WORDE'S EDITION	72

𝕳ere begynneth ye lyf of saynt Ursula after
ye cronycles of englode.

APPENDIX.

	PAGE
HANS MEMLING and the Flemish School of Art—Early Ecclesiastical Paintings—The Byzantine School—The Brothers Van Eyck—Hemling or Memling—The Hospital of John of Bruges—Memling designs the celebrated Shrine of S. Ursula—Religious Art in the Fifteenth Century	103
ROMAN INSCRIPTION FOUND AT COLOGNE	119

INTRODUCTION.

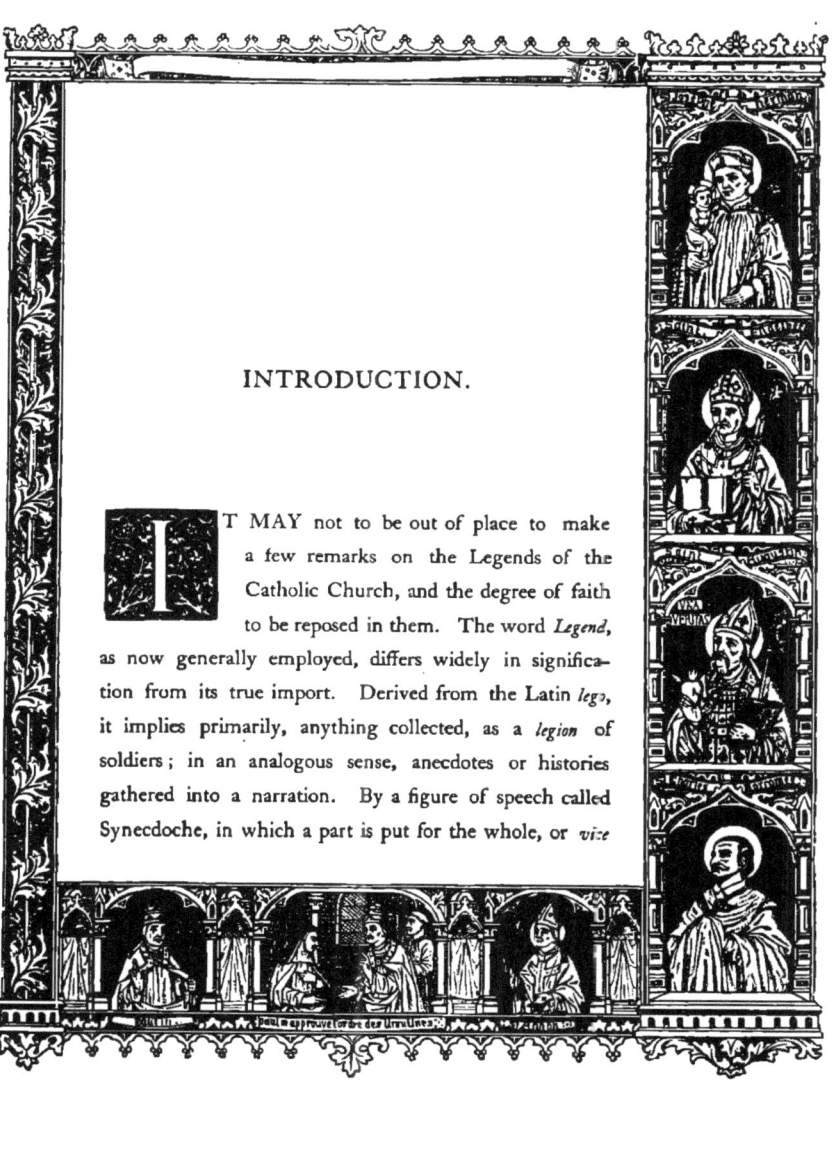

IT MAY not to be out of place to make a few remarks on the Legends of the Catholic Church, and the degree of faith to be reposed in them. The word *Legend*, as now generally employed, differs widely in signification from its true import. Derived from the Latin *lego*, it implies primarily, anything collected, as a *legion* of soldiers; in an analogous sense, anecdotes or histories gathered into a narration. By a figure of speech called Synecdoche, in which a part is put for the whole, or *vice*

INTRODUCTION.

versâ, the word came to mean the reading of the collection: hence legend means simply anything read, or to be read, and is employed in this sense when we speak of the legend of a coin or a seal, meaning the inscription on the exergue. It is probable that the chronicles of the Church were popularly called legends from the circumstance of their being generally read to the brethren at matins and during the time of refection. Whatever may be the true meaning of the word, it must not for a moment be taken in the same sense as a romance or fabulous story.

As to the amount of confidence we are called upon to place in the legends of the Church—are they strictly true in every respect? Undoubtedly not: the Church does not teach us, or require us, to pin our faith implicitly to every detail they record. The great majority of the Church's legends were for many years transmitted orally. The time of the early fathers was usually employed in work more earnest than what may be considered as merely

tombeau de S:Ursule à Cologne.

INTRODUCTION.

ornamental. To them was appointed the task of laying the foundation and erecting the pillars of the Church: it was only in after years that attention could be bestowed upon minor details. It is not, therefore, matter of surprise that traditions thus handed down should, in the course of ages, have suffered some alteration. A common amusement for winter evenings is for a party, perhaps a dozen to seat themselves round a table, and for the first person to whisper a short story to his neighbour, who, in turn, communicates it to the next, and so on until it has travelled completely round. Each person is bound to repeat the story as nearly as possible in the same words in which he received it; but by the time it has reached the last, it is usually found to vary considerably from the original. Thus it is, and must be, with all oral traditions; the main features remain unchanged, though variations unavoidably occur in many of the minor circumstances.

Many persons have attempted to cast discredit on the legend of S. Ursula, urging as an argument against it,

INTRODUCTION.

that it would be impossible for so great a number as eleven thousand virgins to make the journey under the circumstances detailed in the legend. In answer to this we may reply that the church does not say there were eleven thousand; all the brevaries assert is, there was a great number. Herman, Bishop of Cologne, who wrote in the early part of the tenth century, seems to be the first who placed the number at eleven thousand. A century before, Wandalbert thus commemorates the martyrdom of St. Ursula:—

> Tunc numerosa simul Rheni per littora fulgent,
> Christo virgineis erecta trophæa maniplis
> Agrippinæ urbi, quarum furor impius olim
> *Millia* mactavit, ductricibus inclyta sanctis.

Various hypotheses have been put forward to account for the exact number "eleven thousand" having been stated. According to some the number was eleven, and their

INTRODUCTION.

festival was marked in ancient martyrologies XIMV., representing Undecim Martyres Virgines, subsequently understood as Undecimmillia Virgines. Others again suppose that Undecimmillia was the name of one of the principal martyrs, but this is almost too ridiculous to merit serious attention.

In the uncertainty which prevails regarding the exact number of the companions of St. Ursula, we cannot do better than adopt the words of Antonious Page, who, in his *Officia propria sanctorum in Ecclesia cathedralis S. S. Salvatoris et Donatiani*, thus writes, "Earum numerum et nomina, solus ille novit, qui numerat multitudinem stellarum et omnibus eis nomina vocat." 'He only can tell their number and names who counts the multitude of stars, and calls each by its particular appellation.'

Again, it is not to be supposed, as the Rev. Alban Butler remarks, that all the company were unmarried: doubtless amongst the number were many matrons; but, having

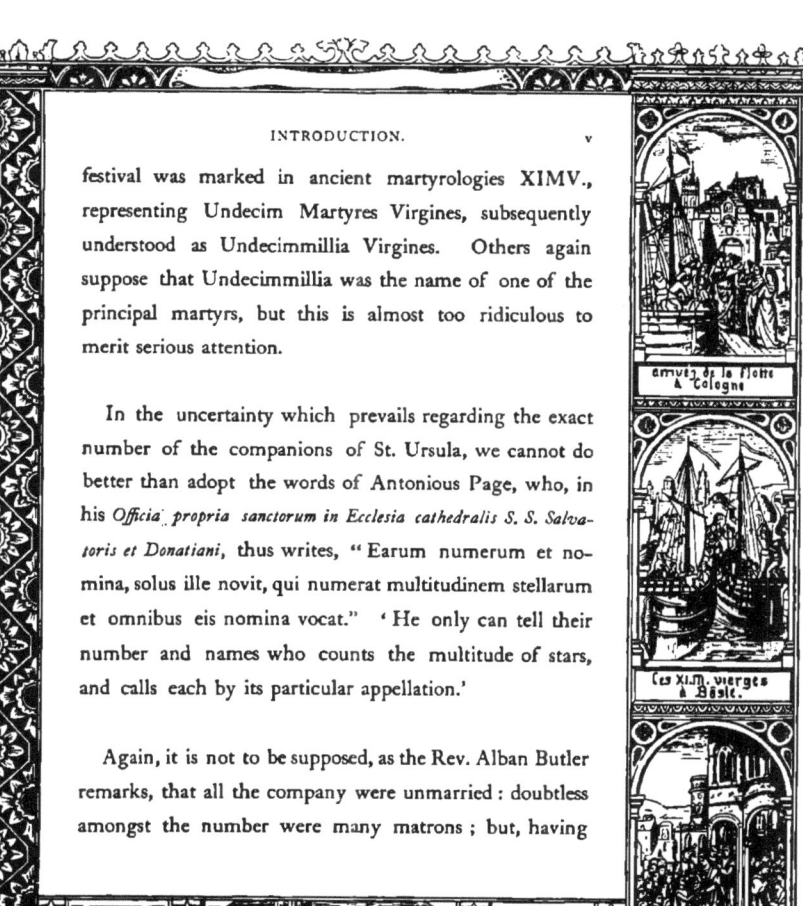

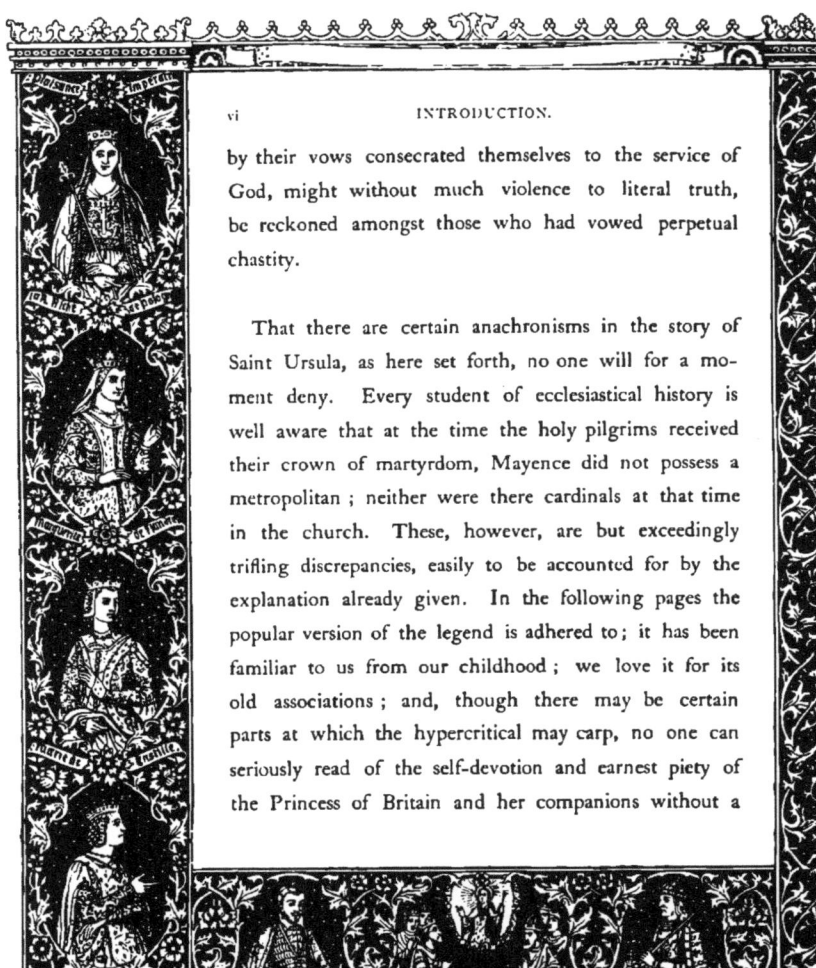

by their vows consecrated themselves to the service of God, might without much violence to literal truth, be reckoned amongst those who had vowed perpetual chastity.

That there are certain anachronisms in the story of Saint Ursula, as here set forth, no one will for a moment deny. Every student of ecclesiastical history is well aware that at the time the holy pilgrims received their crown of martyrdom, Mayence did not possess a metropolitan; neither were there cardinals at that time in the church. These, however, are but exceedingly trifling discrepancies, easily to be accounted for by the explanation already given. In the following pages the popular version of the legend is adhered to; it has been familiar to us from our childhood; we love it for its old associations; and, though there may be certain parts at which the hypercritical may carp, no one can seriously read of the self-devotion and earnest piety of the Princess of Britain and her companions without a feeling of reverence—amounting almost to awe—for those blessed followers of the Lord, who, fighting the good fight of faith, counted not their lives dear unto themselves, so that they might attain everlasting happiness at the end.

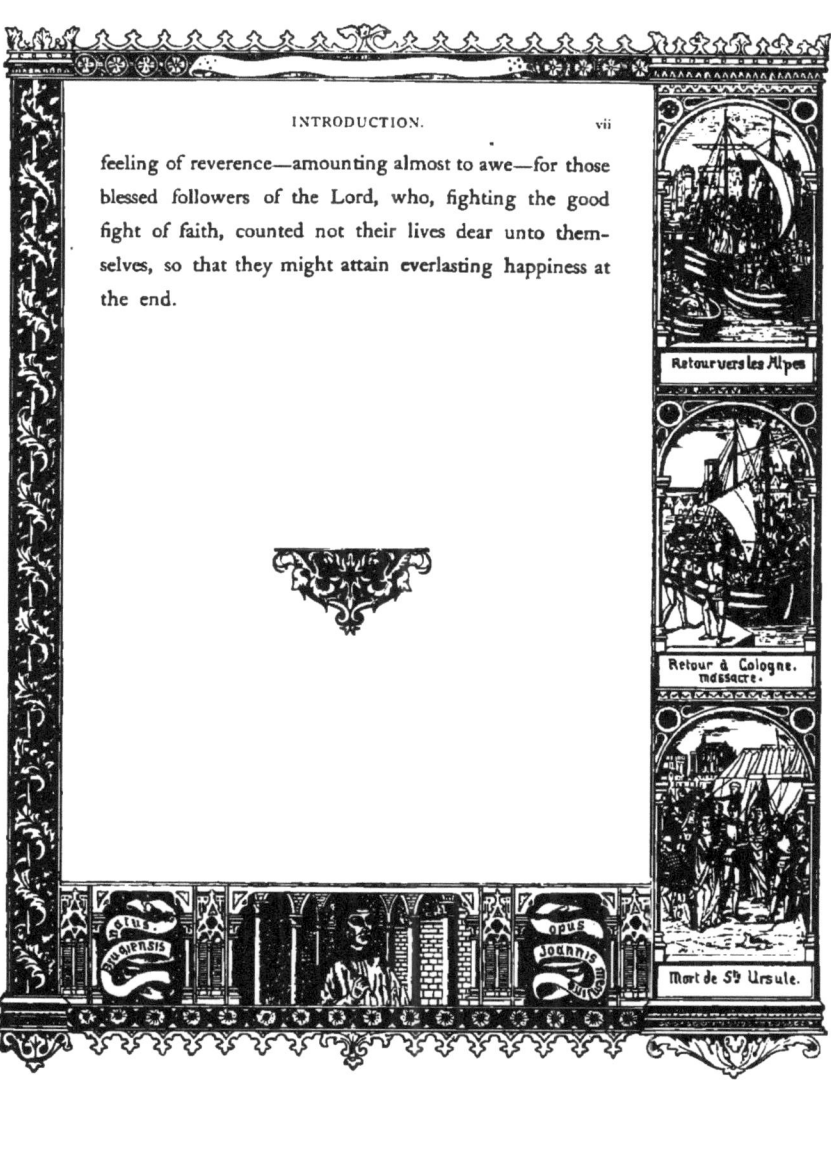

Dominus Deus illuminabit illos ; et regnabunt in secula seculorum : fulgebunt justi sicut sol in regno patris corum.

THE LEGEND OF ST. URSULA.

CHAPTER I.

PARENTAGE OF ST. URSULA—AGRIPPINUS KING OF THE PICTS, AND HIS SON CONAN—EMBASSY TO THE COURT OF DIONOTUS, FATHER OF URSULA, WITH PROPOSALS OF MARRIAGE.

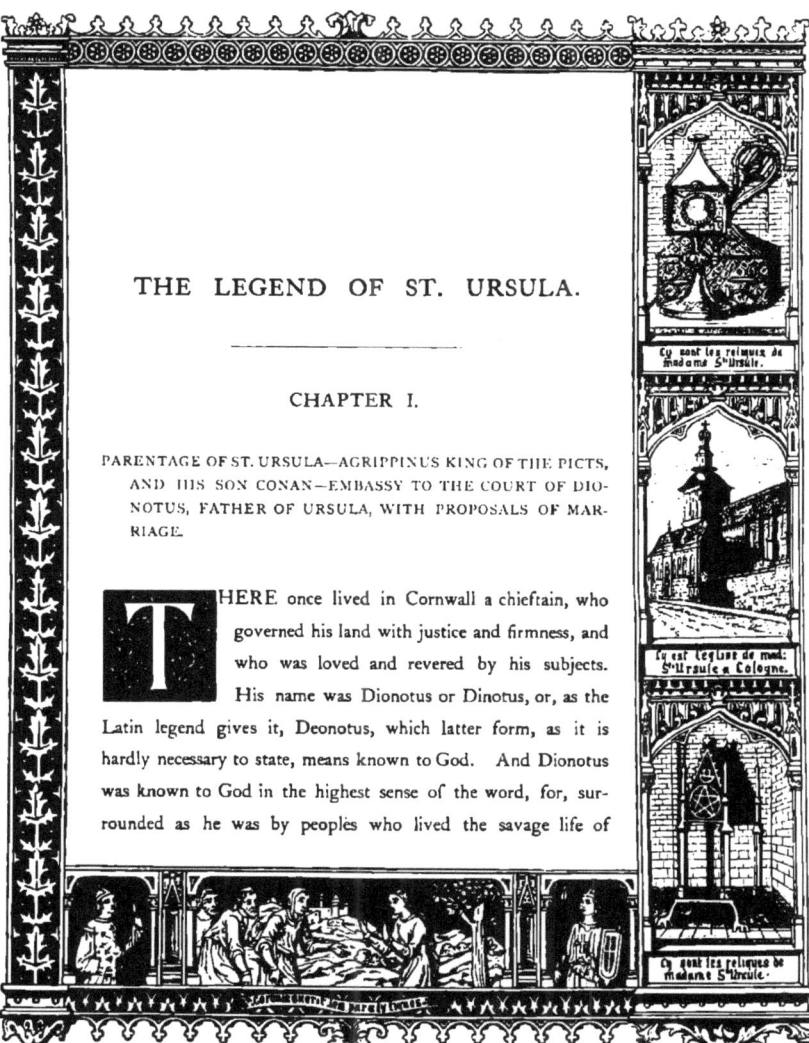

THERE once lived in Cornwall a chieftain, who governed his land with justice and firmness, and who was loved and revered by his subjects. His name was Dionotus or Dinotus, or, as the Latin legend gives it, Deonotus, which latter form, as it is hardly necessary to state, means known to God. And Dionotus was known to God in the highest sense of the word, for, surrounded as he was by peoples who lived the savage life of

THE LEGEND OF ST. URSULA.

pagans, he held the true faith of the Saviour, and was a pious and zealous Catholic, a bright star in the middle of the darkness of a barbarous age. He was thus an example to the people over whom he ruled, who were all good Catholics, like himself, being steady in their belief and practice. Dionotus, too, had a wife who was no less remarkable for her great beauty than for her singular virtue.

God rewarded this exemplary pair by favouring them with a daughter of surpassing beauty, who, moreover, gave promise of the future greatness of her pious merits from her early childhood, and they named her Ursula, a name which, the legend tells us, betokened that in due time she was destined to overcome and strangle the great bear (*ursus*) of evil, or, in other words, Satan himself. Though her father's subjects, exposed as they were to the attacks of inveterate enemies from without, were disappointed in their hopes of a prince who would be their protector and defender after him, yet their discontent was soon appeased by the quick development of the noble qualities of the daughter. In course of time the personal charms of Ursula, and her goodness and piety, were celebrated not only over the domains of Dionotus, but over all Britain, and even beyond its shores.

tombeau de St Ursule à Cologne.

THE LEGEND OF ST. URSULA.

Now Britain was at this time under the power of a pagan king, a great and fierce warrior, who had conquered the land, and reduced it to subjection, and who looked upon the Christians with the greatest hostility. One of the legends styles him Agrippinus. He had a son called Conan, who equalled his father in warlike courage and skill, without possessing his ferocity. Conan listened to the reports of the beauty and gentleness of the Princess Ursula, and being greatly desirous of seeing her, in a stolen visit became so deeply enamoured that he resolved to seek the means of making her his wife.

The king Agrippinus was himself becoming aged, and, still thinking of nothing but warlike expeditions, he placed them under the command of his son, who, like himself, always returned victorious; and he thus became not only the darling of his father, but he was beloved by his warriors as the true and worthy successor of their victorious chieftain. One day, on Conan's triumphant return from a successful expedition, his father sent for him privately into his hall, and there, decked in all the insignia of his rank, he addressed him somewhat as follows:—

THE LEGEND OF ST. URSULA.

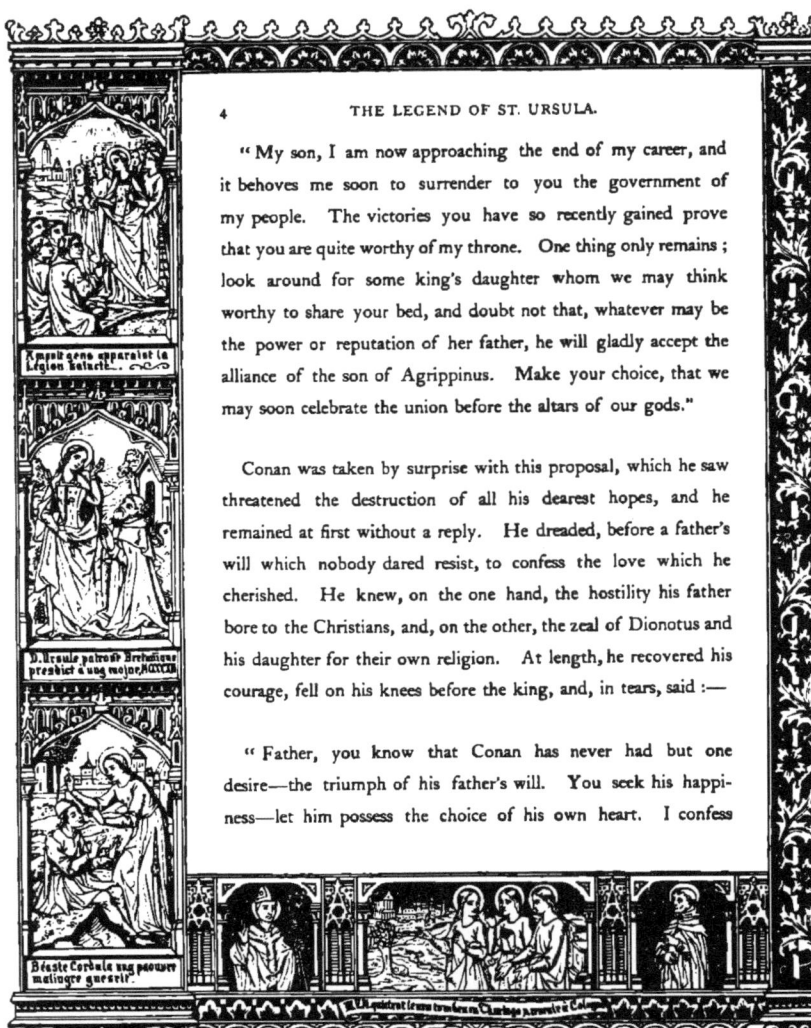

"My son, I am now approaching the end of my career, and it behoves me soon to surrender to you the government of my people. The victories you have so recently gained prove that you are quite worthy of my throne. One thing only remains; look around for some king's daughter whom we may think worthy to share your bed, and doubt not that, whatever may be the power or reputation of her father, he will gladly accept the alliance of the son of Agrippinus. Make your choice, that we may soon celebrate the union before the altars of our gods."

Conan was taken by surprise with this proposal, which he saw threatened the destruction of all his dearest hopes, and he remained at first without a reply. He dreaded, before a father's will which nobody dared resist, to confess the love which he cherished. He knew, on the one hand, the hostility his father bore to the Christians, and, on the other, the zeal of Dionotus and his daughter for their own religion. At length, he recovered his courage, fell on his knees before the king, and, in tears, said:—

"Father, you know that Conan has never had but one desire—the triumph of his father's will. You seek his happiness—let him possess the choice of his own heart. I confess

THE LEGEND OF ST. URSULA.

that that choice is the daughter of one of your enemies; her name is Ursula, and her fame is not unknown in your court. It is true that she despises the power of our gods; but consider that, by combining under one sceptre strength and beauty, you will make your kingdom one of the most powerful states in the world."

The king was moved by Conan's appeal, and he felt in his own way the force of the argument—it was perhaps the only argument which, on such an occasion, he could feel. He probably thought that the religion of the wife was of little importance, if the husband remained firm to that of his forefathers; and, raising his son, he spoke to him cheeringly.

" Let it be, my son," he said, " as you desire; let our ambassadors immediately proceed to the court of Dionotus to demand his daughter, and you will see how gladly he will grant the desire of King Agrippinus."

There were, indeed, many reasons why this alliance should appear very advantageous to Agrippinus himself, for it tended greatly to strengthen the influence of his crown throughout

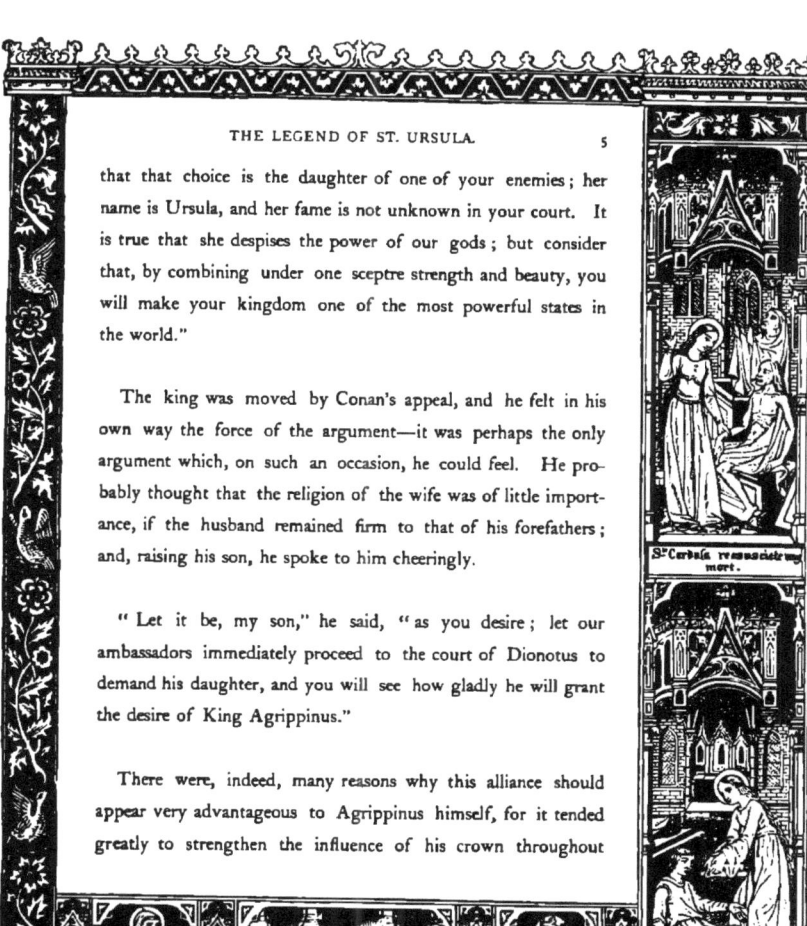

Cy est pourtraicte ma
dame S.te Ursule, et les
Unze Mille vierges:

Britain; and he could hardly suppose that a chieftain so vastly inferior in power to himself as Dionotus would venture to resist him. Politically, too, it was no doubt calculated to raise the position of Dionotus among the petty princes whose territories surrounded his own. Yet Conan trembled, for he was not so sure of the success of the embassy.

Agrippinus left him, and proceeded to join his ministers in the deliberative hall: after a brief consultation, the ambassadors were appointed, and a scribe wrote out the orders by which they were to be guided. The king's desires were to be announced to Dionotus in terms which left him no choice, and the refusal of his daughter would be considered only as a provocation to war. King Agrippinus had never allowed his will to be contradicted.

One of the courtiers, distinguished chiefly as a flatterer, replied that the king might reckon on his servants, after which the council separated.

On the morrow, at break of day, the ten ambassadors were mounted, and ready to take their departure. Amid a crowd of spectators, which covered the place of the palace, they rode forth in pompous attire; and the king, accompanied by his son and by the whole of the court, took leave of them at the palace gate. They were not only armed with threats, but they were also provided with presents and with promises to overcome the objections of Dionotus, before having recourse to the former to work upon his fears.

They were instructed to begin by representing to Dionotus in vivid language the great advantages he would derive from a family alliance with the King of the Picts, and to assure him of the sincerity and friendship sought to be established between them. It was only when those had failed that the ambassadors were to threaten him with hostility.

The reliquary of the holy Lady St. Ursula.

CHAPTER II.

THE AMBASSADORS OF AGRIPPINUS REACH THE COURT OF
DIONOTUS, AND RECEIVE HIS REPLY TO THEIR MESSAGE.

IN those days travelling was slow, and the journey from the court of Agrippinus to that of Dionotus was accordingly a long one, but the ambassadors, accompanied by an imposing retinue, arrived in due time, and presented their credentials. They were received honorably, and were listened to with attention. Their spokesman began by boasting of the greatness and power of King Agrippinus, and representing in persuasive language the advantages which would arise to Dionotus from the matrimonial alliance he proposed; but, finding that such

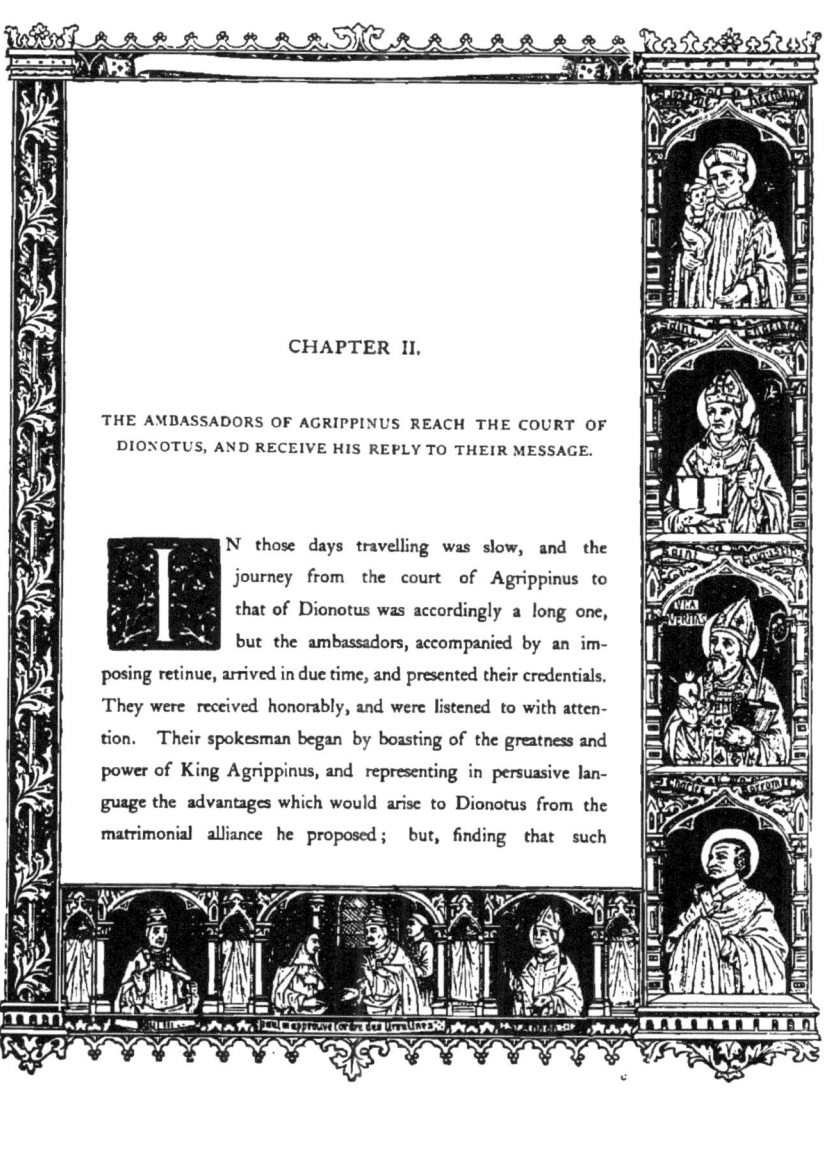

THE LEGEND OF ST. URSULA.

arguments produced but little effect, he had recourse to threats, and pointed out in impressive terms the ruin and destruction with which the kingdom of Cornwall was threatened, if it should provoke the anger of the great and victorious king of the north.

Dionotus was entirely unprepared for this proposal, which was altogether contrary to his own sentiments, and for a moment he remained silent. On one side, how could he yield up his beloved daughter, whose heart was given up only to the love of her Heavenly Lord, to the embraces of a heathen and a barbarian? On the other, he was too conscious of his temporal weakness and of his utter inability to resist the forces and warlike skill of his northern antagonist, and he saw only in the future his country laid waste, his subjects slaughtered, their wives and daughters given up to the savage lust of their enemies, and, worse than all, the altars of their holy religion polluted, and their churches abandoned to the flames. Distracted mentally by the consideration of these conflicted reasons, Dionotus remained for some time silent, and then, recovering his self-possession, he told the ambassadors that he felt unprepared to give an immediate answer to a proposal which came upon him so suddenly, and

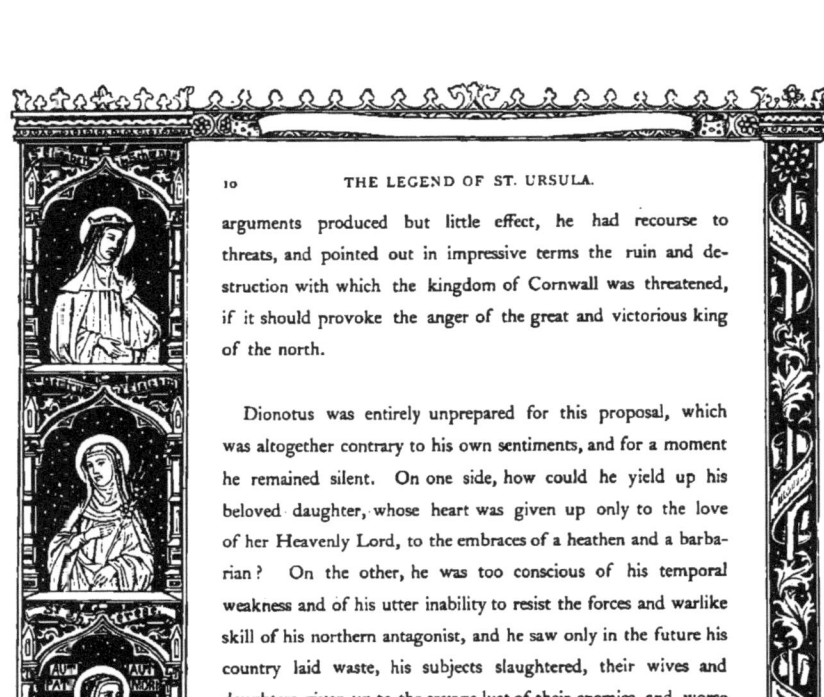

THE LEGEND OF ST. URSULA.

which was to himself of such great importance, and he said that he felt it above all things necessary to consult the will of the young princess herself before giving a decisive reply. It was thus agreed that a certain space of time should be allowed for reflection and negotiation, during which the envoys of the pagan king were treated with the greatest consideration.

It is not difficult to imagine the anxiety which, during this interval, tortured the hearts of the noble-minded father and pious mother of the Princess Ursula. Days and nights, almost without intermission, were spent in humble prayer to heaven for assistance in this great difficulty, and no one prayed more fervently than Ursula herself, who had been informed of the object of this extraordinary embassy, and, in her compassion for the troubles thus brought upon her parents, had signified her entire submission to their will. She gave herself up to her devotions with such extreme fervour, that the change which quickly appeared in her complexion and strength seemed to announce that she was hastening to that country where the persecutions of the wicked possess force no longer.

At length the eve of the fatal day arrived, and the maiden,

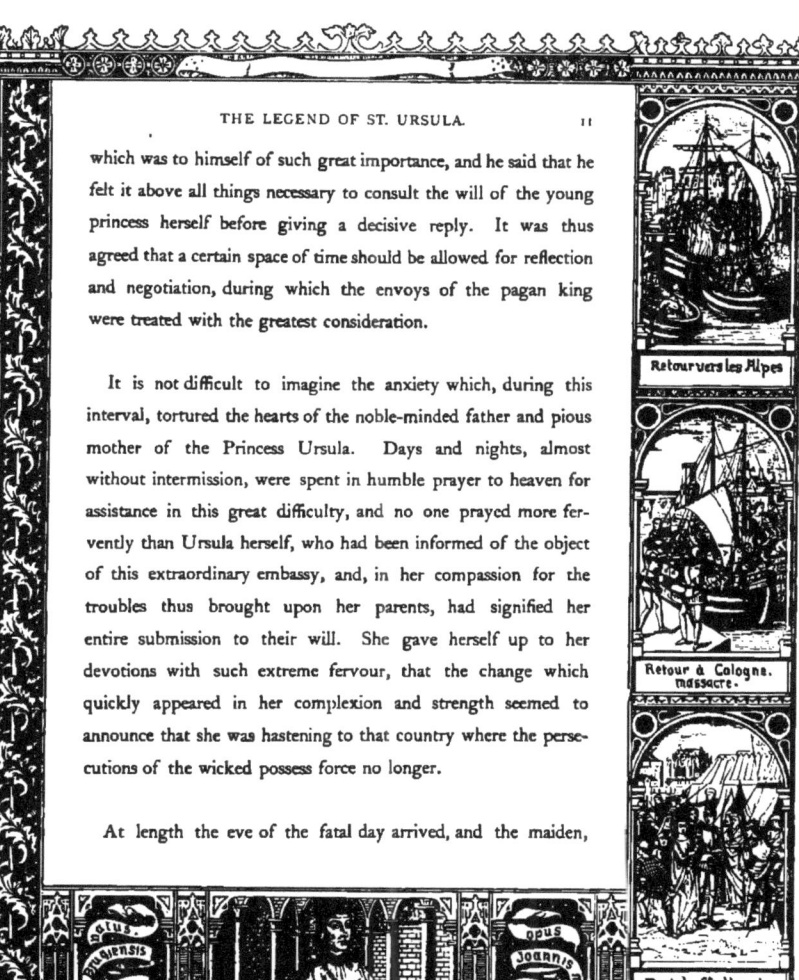

THE LEGEND OF ST. URSULA.

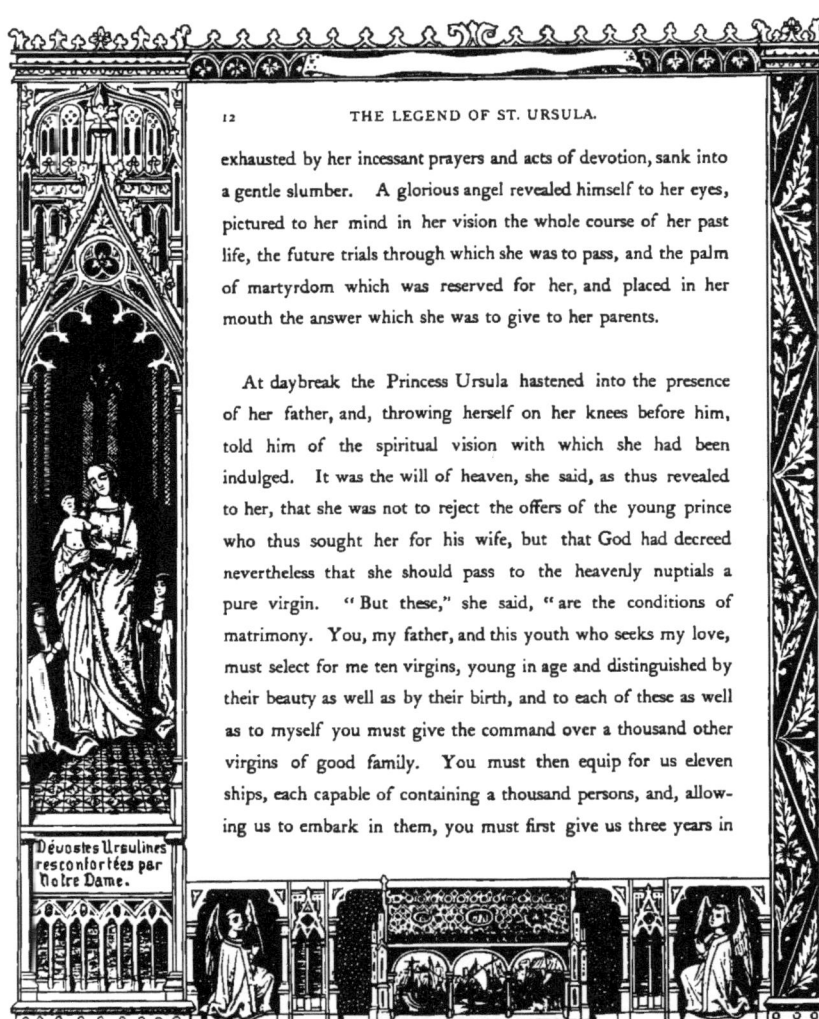

Dévostes Ursulines resconfortées par Notre Dame.

exhausted by her incessant prayers and acts of devotion, sank into a gentle slumber. A glorious angel revealed himself to her eyes, pictured to her mind in her vision the whole course of her past life, the future trials through which she was to pass, and the palm of martyrdom which was reserved for her, and placed in her mouth the answer which she was to give to her parents.

At daybreak the Princess Ursula hastened into the presence of her father, and, throwing herself on her knees before him, told him of the spiritual vision with which she had been indulged. It was the will of heaven, she said, as thus revealed to her, that she was not to reject the offers of the young prince who thus sought her for his wife, but that God had decreed nevertheless that she should pass to the heavenly nuptials a pure virgin. " But these," she said, " are the conditions of matrimony. You, my father, and this youth who seeks my love, must select for me ten virgins, young in age and distinguished by their beauty as well as by their birth, and to each of these as well as to myself you must give the command over a thousand other virgins of good family. You must then equip for us eleven ships, each capable of containing a thousand persons, and, allowing us to embark in them, you must first give us three years in

THE LEGEND OF ST. URSULA.

which to dedicate our virginities to God. At the expiration of that period, let his will be done. At the same time be assured that nothing in this world can avert the fulfilment of God's designs in regard to thy daughter."

The hearts of King Dionotus and his nobles were relieved and rejoiced by this divine revelation, and tears of happiness were the only language which announced their feelings. The king immediately proceeded to his council chamber, and summoned the ambassadors to his presence. He there announced to them the conditions of marriage which the princess required, and added that the virgin desired further that, during the three years of delay required by the vision, the young prince Conan should allow himself to be instructed in the Christian faith, and that, if possible, he should submit to the rite of baptism.

Meanwhile, God had so far worked upon the minds of the ambassadors and their heathen countrymen that, instead of expressing any dissatisfaction at such an announcement, they received it gladly as a sufficient reply to their embassy, and returned home to the court of Agrippinus, whose subjects received the intelligence with the utmost joy. The king and the young

prince Conan subscribed to the conditions willingly, and the latter expressed an eager desire to be initiated without further delay into the mysteries of Christianity.

CHAPTER III.

OF THE BUILDING OF THE SHIPS AND THE SELECTION OF THE VIRGINS, AND OF THEIR EXERCISES.

THE two kings were now united in friendship, and it was agreed that, during the three years of proof enjoined by the divine revelation, the Prince Conan was to undergo a course of instruction in the Christian faith. The next step in carrying out the will of heaven was the building of eleven ships, each to carry a thousand virgins. This work demanded only labour and skill, for the country was at this time covered with vast forests, which reached down to the shores, and timber was plentiful, and ready at

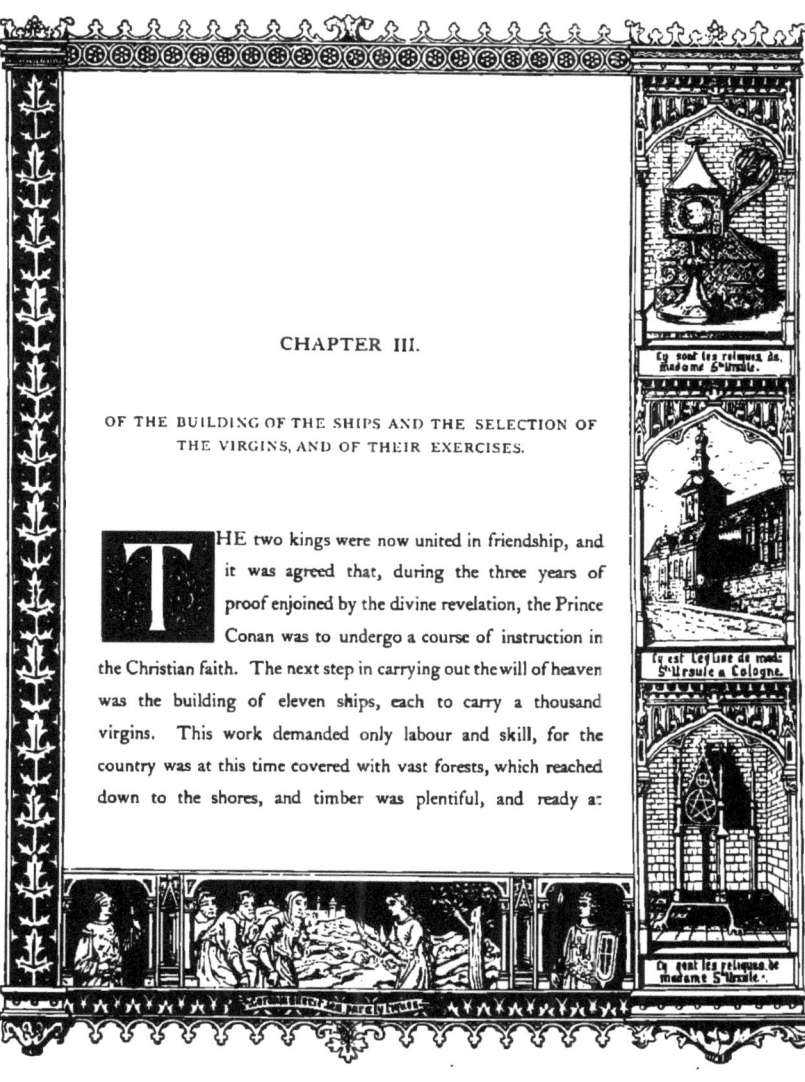

16   THE LEGEND OF ST. URSULA.

hand. The place was soon chosen for a ship-yard, and stocks were erected for the required number of vessels. Men skilled in ship-building were brought together from all parts of the island, for the princes in Britain now encouraged the undertaking, and the work thus proceeded steadily and rapidly.

The beauty no less than the dignity of the princess, for whom, in the first place, they were working, the popularity of her royal father, the interest taken in their labours by the kings of Britain, and above all the divine influence, inspired the breasts of the workmen with zeal.

From time to time Ursula, accompanied by her father Dionotus, visited them in person, and encouraged them by their exhortations. In their route, which was facilitated by the clearing of the forests through the immense quantities of timber cut down for the construction of the ships, Dionotus listened to the pious conversations of his daughter, and in return instructed her in the management of fleets, as well as in the government of numerous bodies of people, such as were to be confided to her care. Arrived at the scene of labour, they examined every part of the works, praised the skill of the workmen, and rewarded

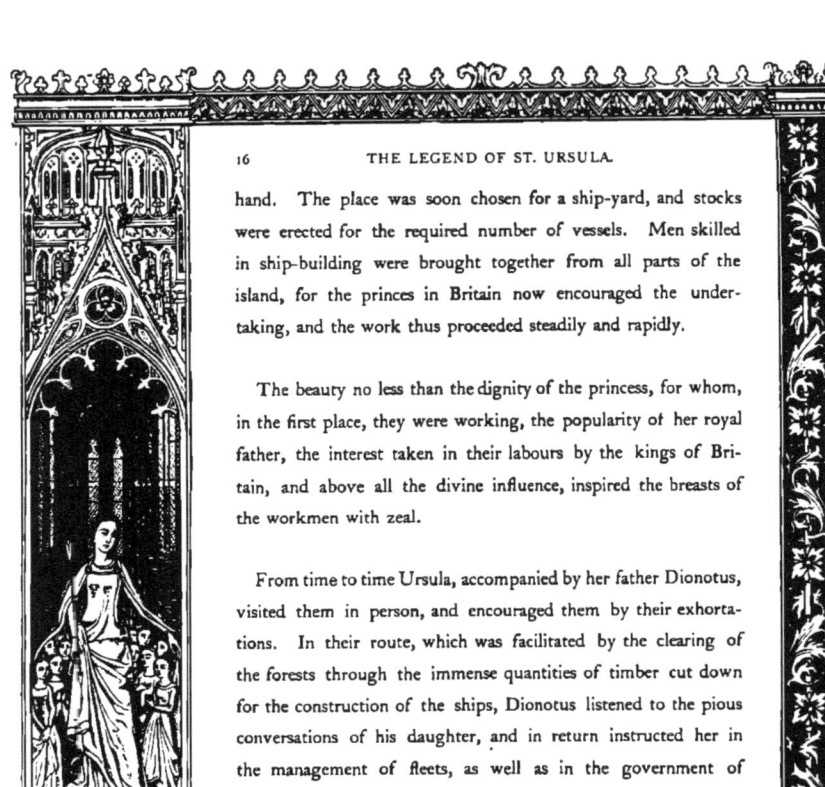

THE LEGEND OF ST. URSULA.

them for their zeal, and they were received with the profound respect which their noble and kindly bearing impressed upon all.

During this time, no efforts were spared to collect together the number of devoted maidens which was enjoined in the revelation. Among the most zealous of Conan's co-adjutors in this task was his favourite sister, whom Ursula received into her arms with the warmest affection, and whom she made her second in command over the virgin cohorts. The ancient legend gives her the name of Pinnosa, but the name is varied in the different versions of the story. She brought with her sixteen hundred and forty virgins, all young, and selected from the most illustrious families of the nation of the Picts.

Two queens of the Caledonians, both of the same lineage as Agrippina and Conan, were equally zealous in the cause, and sought recruits among the noblest and fairest daughters of their country. Twelve hundred and thirty-two Caledonian virgins joined the standard of the Princess Ursula, and arrived at the court of Dionotus to swell the ranks of her army of saints. They were accompanied by a lady whom the legends call Hilmegardis, who had just been espoused to a noble warrior, and possessed all the

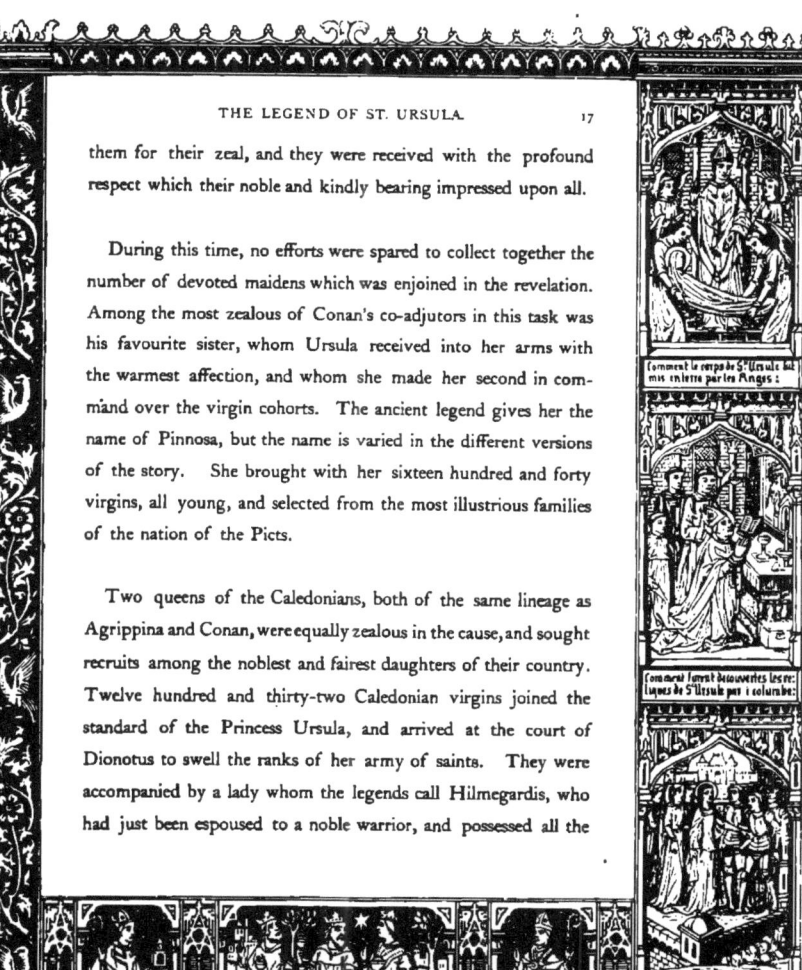

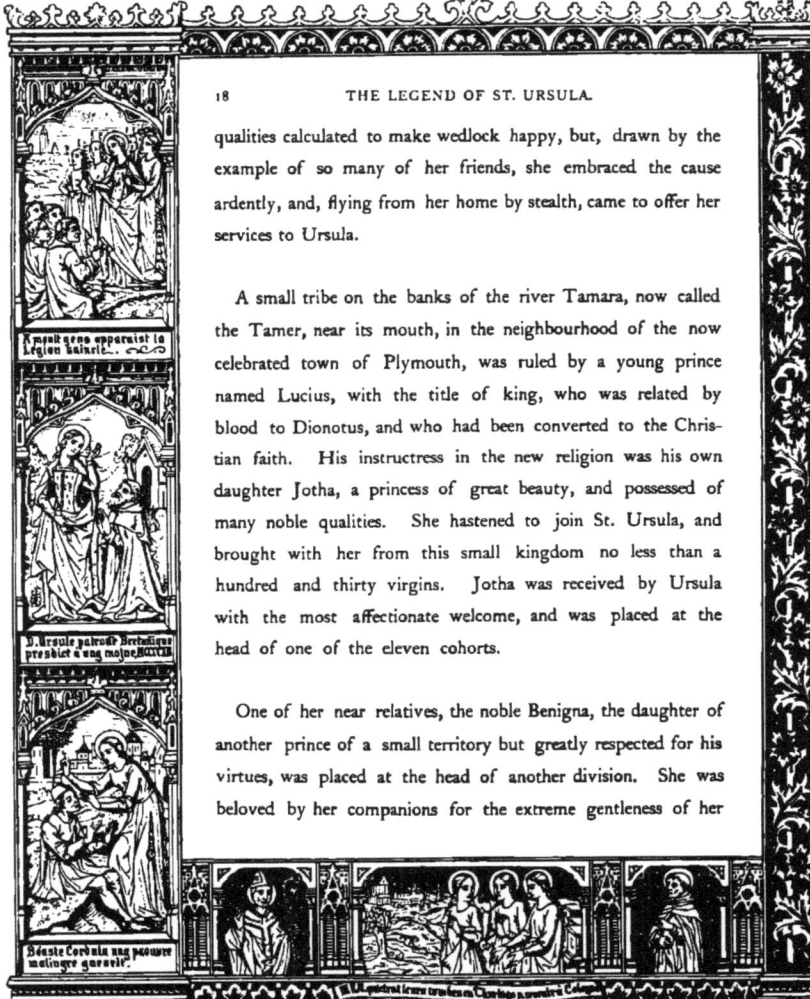

qualities calculated to make wedlock happy, but, drawn by the example of so many of her friends, she embraced the cause ardently, and, flying from her home by stealth, came to offer her services to Ursula.

A small tribe on the banks of the river Tamara, now called the Tamer, near its mouth, in the neighbourhood of the now celebrated town of Plymouth, was ruled by a young prince named Lucius, with the title of king, who was related by blood to Dionotus, and who had been converted to the Christian faith. His instructress in the new religion was his own daughter Jotha, a princess of great beauty, and possessed of many noble qualities. She hastened to join St. Ursula, and brought with her from this small kingdom no less than a hundred and thirty virgins. Jotha was received by Ursula with the most affectionate welcome, and was placed at the head of one of the eleven cohorts.

One of her near relatives, the noble Benigna, the daughter of another prince of a small territory but greatly respected for his virtues, was placed at the head of another division. She was beloved by her companions for the extreme gentleness of her

THE LEGEND OF ST. URSULA.

disposition, and her command over her companions was exercised rather by her example than by her orders.

Avitus was the king of a people called the Danmonians, who occupied the territory round the present city of Exeter. He sent to Ursula his daughter Columba, and his niece Odilia, both betrothed to princes of distinction, but they preferred the services of heaven to all other ties, and embraced the cause of the princess Ursula with the greatest ardour. She placed each of them at the head of one of her bands of virgins.

The modest Chilindris, the daughter of a noble warrior, the intimate friend of the prince last mentioned, was also placed in command as a reward for her many virtues.

Another prince zealous in the cause, Siranus, king of Ischalis—the modern Ilchester—was the near kinsman of Ursula's mother. He brought to her a detachment of a hundred and eighty young and illustrious beauties, who entered her service with earnest zeal. One of them, who is named in the legend Sibilia, was also appointed to the command of a division.

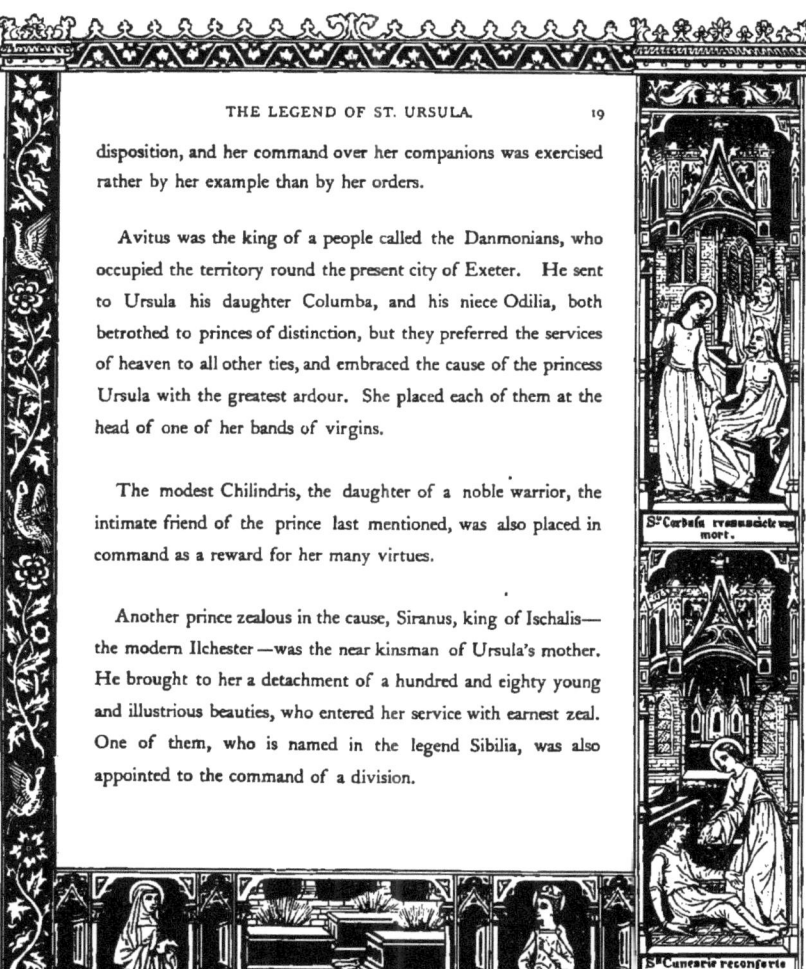

It would be long to enumerate all the names which the legends have preserved for praise among the extraordinary host, as remarkable above the rest for their virtue equally as for their personal beauties, three of whom, are also mentioned as having been placed at the head of cohorts.

A number of holy and eloquent bishops embraced the cause, and promoted it by their zealous preaching. Many venerable matrons also attached themselves to their daughters and nieces. And several princes abandoned their claims to terrestrial thrones, to follow the steps of those on whom they had cast their love, in order to offer them protection in their voyage. A certain number, who were distinguished by their pure and virtuous lives, were allowed to share in their dangers. Two of these, who were own brothers, and named in the legend Canut and Evodius, were the lovers of the high-bearing maiden Luminosa and of the modest Cordula. Both of them were the chosen companions and counsellors of St. Ursula herself.

As each new party of recruits arrived, the king, dressed in his robes of ceremony, with his crown on his head, issued from his palace to receive them with honour, and led them to his

tombeau de S:t Ursule à Cologne.

THE LEGEND OF ST. URSULA.

daughter, their pious leader. She received them with a simplicity and gentleness which at once attached them to her person, and addressed them with an eloquence so winning that it gained all their hearts. They were then led to the habitations which had been prepared for them, where they occupied their time in prayer and meditation, awaiting the moment when they were to be called forth to take their part in more active labours.

Retour vers les Alpes

Having appointed the commanders of all the ten cohorts of her army of maidens, she called them together several times a week, to practise them in spiritual as well as in bodily exercise. Having drawn them up in order around her, she addressed prayers to God imploring his guidance and direction in all their proceedings, and prepared them by her exhortations against the dangers of whatever kind they were destined to encounter in their voyage. When the company of virgins were thus strengthened in their hearts by spiritual exercises, Ursula led them to the shore, and they sprang with joy on board their ships which awaited them there. Then they all rushed with alacrity to their work;—some hoisted the masts, others worked upon the ropes, and spread the sails, while others again put their hands to the oars, and all with wonderful order and skill. It seemed

Retour à Cologne.
massacre.

Mort de Ste Ursule.

THE LEGEND OF ST. URSULA.

as though all these young damsels were suddenly inspired with the most perfect skill in naval discipline and instruction.

What was still more extraordinary, all this was done without the assistance or teaching of any one of the other sex. Their own hands were the only instruments. Soon the ships moved out to sea, formed now in close line, and now separated, feigning flight or pursuit, turned to the starboard, turned to the larboard, and practised other manœuvres, and all with marvellous accuracy and rapidity. Ursula herself, without assistance, guided the movements of her own vessel, and displayed a skill superior to the rest.

The king, and his family and court, were usually assembled on the shore to witness these extraordinary naval reviews. They were held, according to the state of the tide, sometimes in the morning, and sometimes later, in the middle of the day; and sometimes they were prolonged from morning to eve. When they came in front of a favourable harbour, Ursula would give the signal for casting anchor, and for a few instants put into port. And then the king would come and address them with words of encouragement, and would sometimes add instructions in the management of their ships and in the art of navigation.

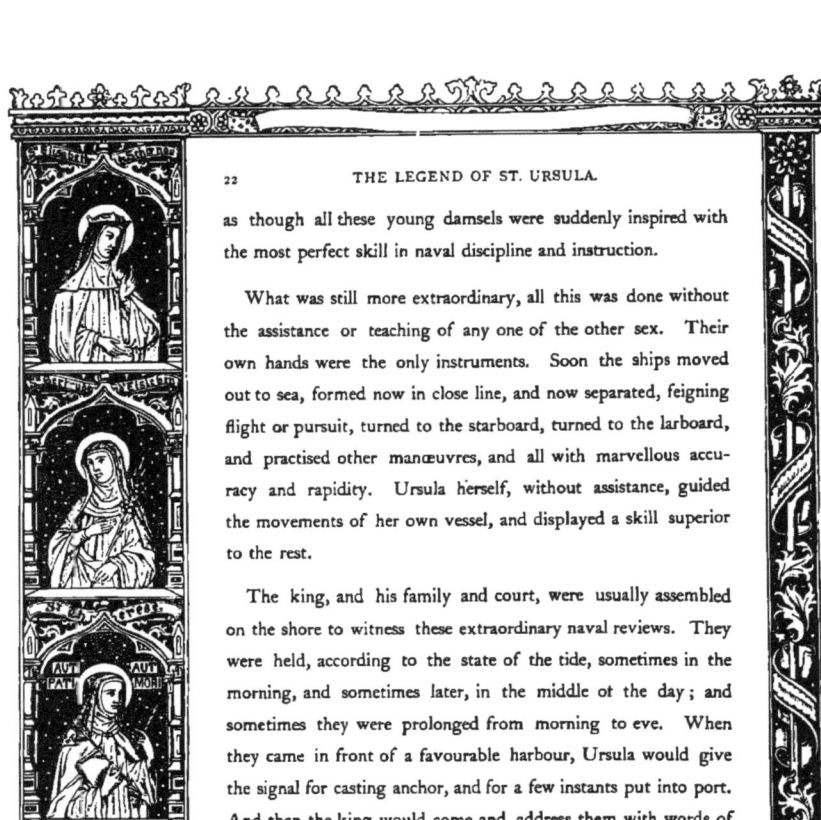

THE LEGEND OF ST. URSULA.

The rendezvous of the fleet was always the same spacious and safe harbour at the mouth of the Tamara; and as they approached it on their return from these exercises, a thousand fair virgins crowded the deck of each, and sent up to heaven their loud chaunt of praise.

Dévostes Ursulines resconfortées par Notre Dame.

CHAPTER IV.

DEPARTURE OF THE FLEET; THEY ARE CARRIED TO THIEL
IN HOLLAND, AND PROCEED THENCE TO COLOGNE.

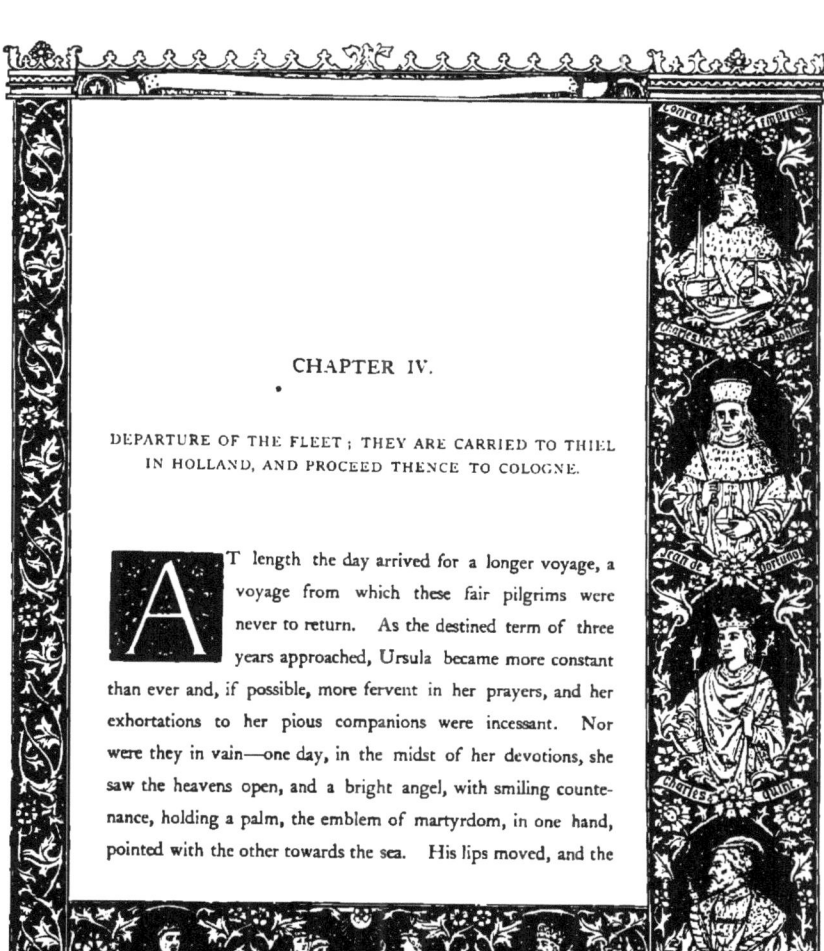

AT length the day arrived for a longer voyage, a voyage from which these fair pilgrims were never to return. As the destined term of three years approached, Ursula became more constant than ever and, if possible, more fervent in her prayers, and her exhortations to her pious companions were incessant. Nor were they in vain—one day, in the midst of her devotions, she saw the heavens open, and a bright angel, with smiling countenance, holding a palm, the emblem of martyrdom, in one hand, pointed with the other towards the sea. His lips moved, and the

26   THE LEGEND OF ST. URSULA.

following words fell upon the ears of the princess. "Blessed maiden, at daybreak to-morrow embark in your ships, and heaven will be with you." Ursula was astonished and troubled, and for a while remained in a trance. Then, as the vision had disappeared, she arose, and repaired to her parents and to her companions, and informed them of the joyful intelligence. They rejoiced with her, and the last preparations for departure were made in silence. The ships were provisioned for a voyage of which no one knew the duration.

At the first break of day-light the fleet rode at anchor at the mouth of the Tamara ready for sailing. Ursula and her companions were soon embarked, the anchors drawn, and the sails raised. King Dionotus, with his nobles and virtuous queen, had come to give them their blessings and bid them adieu. The former sought to encourage his daughter by manifesting a feeling of saintly joy, and by uttering a few words of encouragement. Ursula herself is clad in the purple garb of royalty; she embraces the king affectionately, then mounts on board her ship, and gives the signal for departure.

Slowly the ships left the harbour, and, impelled only by the

THE LEGEND OF ST. URSULA.

force of the oars, kept near to the shore for a short distance, and then made for the open sea. Ursula ordered the sails to be spread to the wind, and then a gentle gale arose, breathing a pleasant temperature and sound as though it came from heaven, filled the sails, and drove the ships forward smoothly and pleasantly. They have lost sight of the coast of England, and move forward they know not whither. Yet joy is in their hearts, and they testify it by chaunting songs of thankfulness.

After a time the wind changes, and they are carried towards the north. That day and the night following they wandered over the sea, at God's will, and under his direction. At daybreak, new coasts arose to their astonished eyes, and they rapidly approached the wide mouth of a spacious river. It led them into the Wahalis, the modern Waal, one of the principal rivers of ancient Batavia, which we now call Holland.

A land to them unknown lay around them, and seemed to rise out of the bosom of the waves. The shores on both sides were covered with towns and palaces, and with meadows, and fields, and woods. As the ships moved along the surface of the water, the wind continually changed its direction so as to

arrivez de la Flotte à Cologne

Les XI.M. vierges à Basle.

D. Ursule et ses comp.s à Rome.

28 THE LEGEND OF ST. URSULA.

accommodate itself to the sinuosities of the river, and they threaded its course with safety, without any efforts of their own.

At length a fine city appears, spreading itself along the bank of the river. It was the town of Tiele, now called Thiele, the great mart of Batavia in ancient times, and Ursula and her companions beheld its quays covered with a crowd of merchants and strangers, for it was the period of one of their great fairs. Ursula felt within her a consciousness that this was to be her first resting place, and she gave the signal for her fleet to cast anchor.

The sudden appearance of so many ships, bearing so unusual a cargo, naturally excited the astonishment and curiosity of the crowds on shore. Among them were merchants from the great and flourishing city of the Ubii, to which the Romans, who had raised it to that highest rank of municpality which was termed a colony, had given the name of Colonia Agrippina, and which we now call Cologne. These merchants had some how or other obtained information that the numerous virgins who filled the ships they saw before them were natives of Britain, and they put

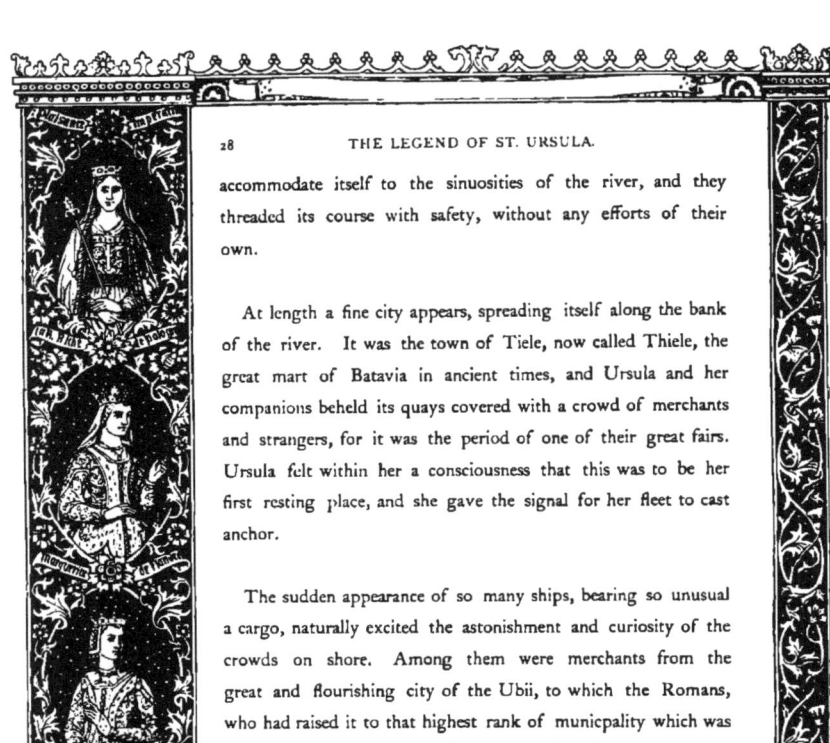

THE LEGEND OF ST. URSULA.

off from the shore, and presented themselves on board the ship which was directed by Ursula herself. They were received with friendly welcome, and they informed her that there dwelt in their city a princess of the same race as herself, that her name was Sigillindis, and that she greatly edified the citizens by the holiness of her life. Ursula recognized in this message the voice of heaven, and she determined on proceeding immediately to Cologne.

But, first, the holy bishops of Britain, who had accompanied Ursula on her voyage, landed at Thiel, and informed the clergy of that city of the arrival of the illustrious voyageurs, and also of the circumstances of their voyage. Immediately the Bishop of Batavia, whose see was at Thiel, with his deacons and acolytes, proceeded to the port to offer their salutations to the noble British princess and the legion of damsels who accompanied her, to pray for the full accomplishment of their vows, and to give them a parting benediction.

As I have said, there resided at this time at Cologne a princely British lady named Sigillindis. She was a widow, still in the flower of youth, and shared a modest dwelling on the Greesberg,

a hill near the city with a priest named Quirillus, the same whose name is attached, as author, to the relation of the subsequent massacre of Ursula and her companions. The residence of Sigillindis and Quirillus was sanctified by the possession of the precious relics of the holy St. Magdalene.

One day when Sigillindis was plunged in saintly meditations, and was holding communion with the heavenly angels, it was revealed to her that a numerous host of virgins, led by a pious princess, had left the coast of Britain on their way to Rome, that they would visit Cologne on their way, and that they would return thither to confirm their devotion to God's will and merit the crown of martydom. She was enjoined to accompany the virgins to Rome, and to share in their future adventures.

Ursula had disembarked, and passed the night in the city of Thiel, with the determination to proceed on her voyage next day. At daybreak she was at the port with her companions, and they again went on board their ships, and the anchors were raised. They directed their course up the river, then difficult of navigation ; but the same mysterious wind which had directed them hitherto, re-appeared, and carried them forward gently and

Tombeau de S.te Ursule à Cologne.

THE LEGEND OF ST. URSULA.

safely. They passed the town then called Noviomagus, now Nimeguen, the border-town of the Roman empire in this direction, and soon afterwards were carried into the majestic waters of the Rhine. A short space of time brought them under the walls of the famous city of Cologne.

As the temples and porticoes of the Roman city present themselves to the view, the wind falls, the sails slacken, and the ship guided by Ursula herself first touches the port, near the Capitol, the walls of which were bathed by the waters of the river. The gates of the Basilica are opened, and the archbishop descends the steps of the temple, and proceeds to the shore of the river to receive the distinguished visitors. Salutations are exchanged in the name of God and of Holy Church, and then, with chaunts of joy, Ursula and her companions are led to the church to render thanks to heaven for their safe and prosperous voyage.

Under the directions of the archbishop and of the pious Sigillindis, lodgings were provided in Cologne for the virgins from Britain. All the Christians of the city came forward to offer them a tender welcome; and Sigillindis, with the assist-

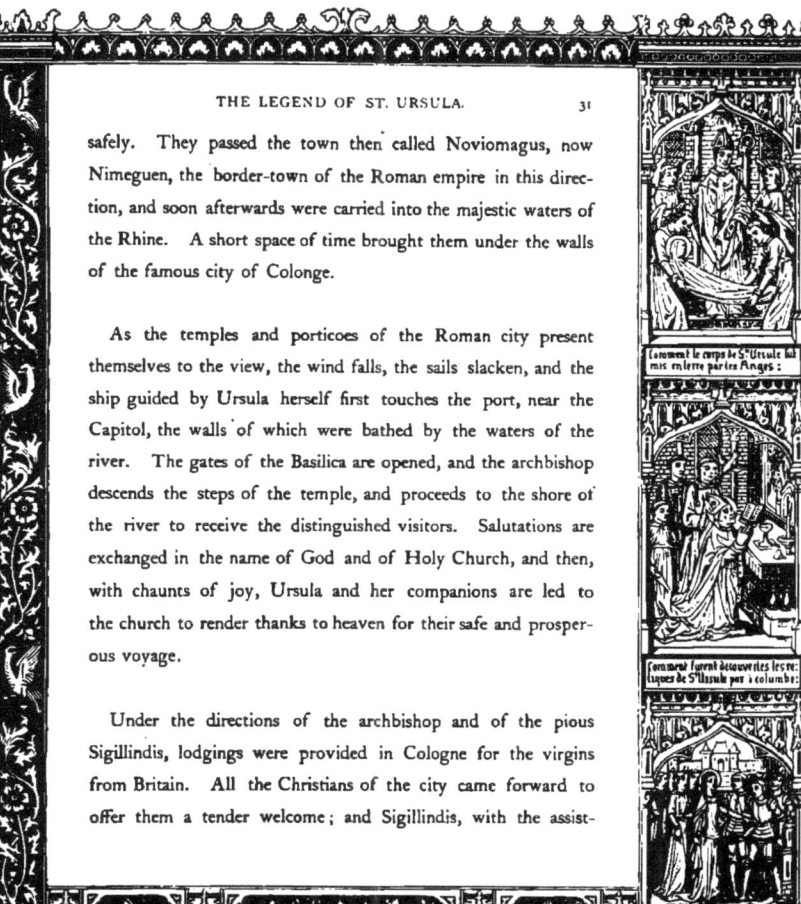

THE LEGEND OF ST. URSULA.

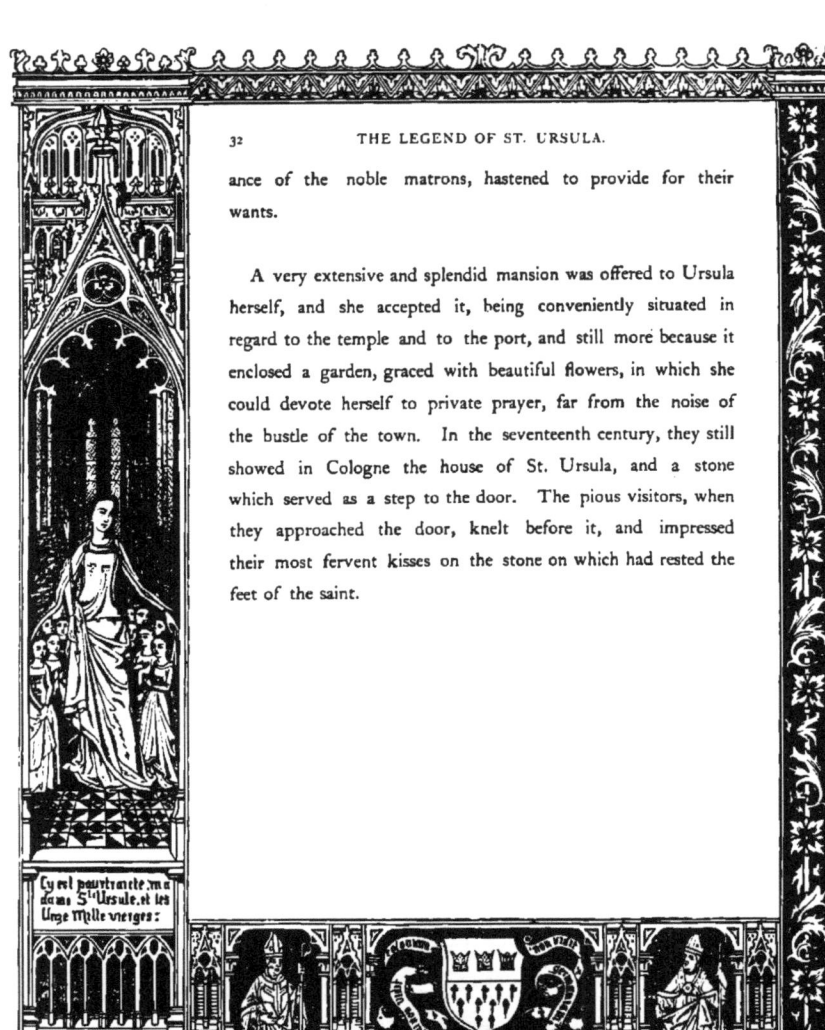

ance of the noble matrons, hastened to provide for their wants.

A very extensive and splendid mansion was offered to Ursula herself, and she accepted it, being conveniently situated in regard to the temple and to the port, and still more because it enclosed a garden, graced with beautiful flowers, in which she could devote herself to private prayer, far from the noise of the bustle of the town. In the seventeenth century, they still showed in Cologne the house of St. Ursula, and a stone which served as a step to the door. The pious visitors, when they approached the door, knelt before it, and impressed their most fervent kisses on the stone on which had rested the feet of the saint.

CHAPTER V.

URSULA'S VISION; HER VISIT TO ROME.

IN the garden of her house in Cologne, Ursula knelt in prayer, and implored the Lord to support her in her coming trials, and to make her acquainted with his will. The necessity of sleep, caused in part by the fatigues of the voyage, came over her, and she retired to her chamber, and threw herself upon a couch; but her eyes were hardly closed, when she was aroused by a voice which uttered the words, "Ursula! Ursula!" She opened her eyes, and saw a beautiful angel leaning against the window. Overcome with dread, she raised herself on the couch, and,

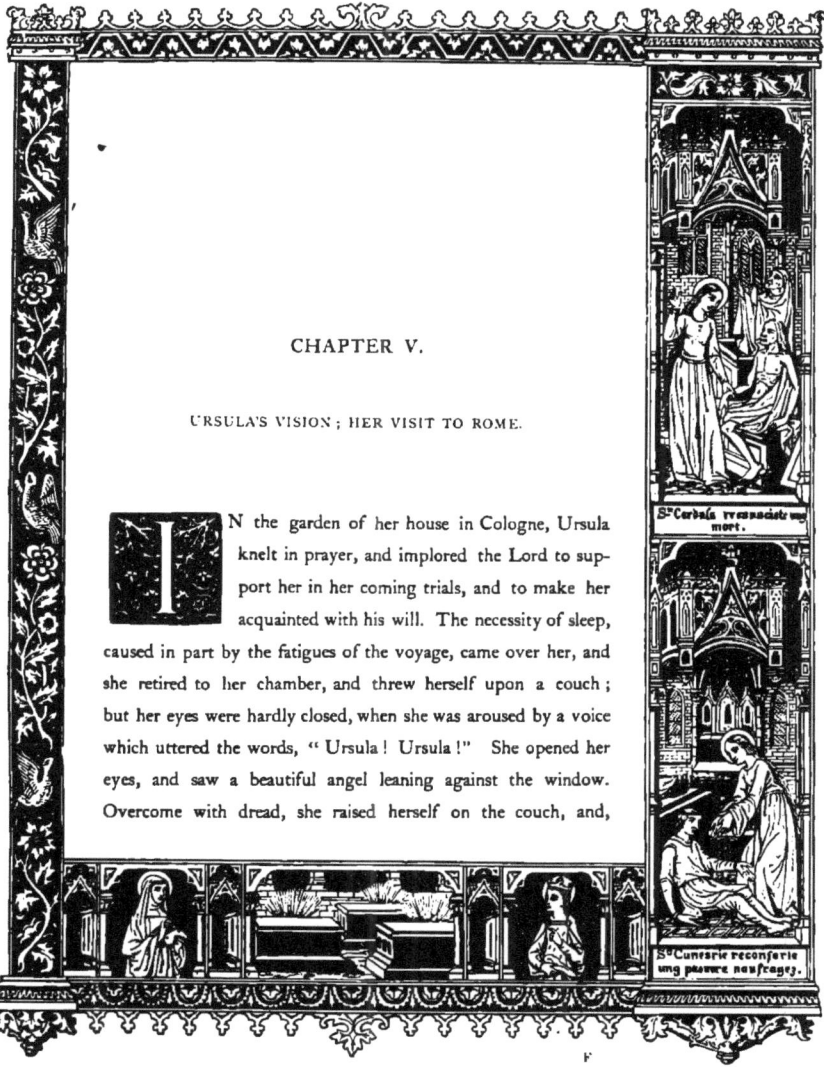

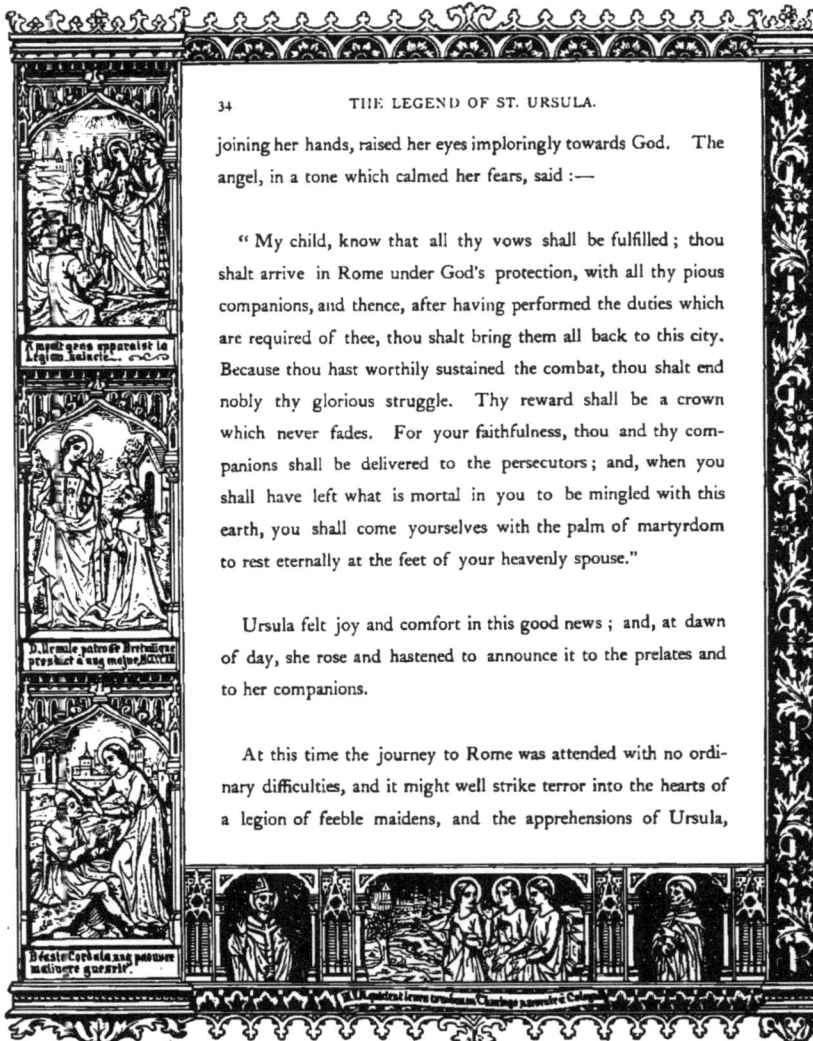

joining her hands, raised her eyes imploringly towards God. The angel, in a tone which calmed her fears, said:—

"My child, know that all thy vows shall be fulfilled; thou shalt arrive in Rome under God's protection, with all thy pious companions, and thence, after having performed the duties which are required of thee, thou shalt bring them all back to this city. Because thou hast worthily sustained the combat, thou shalt end nobly thy glorious struggle. Thy reward shall be a crown which never fades. For your faithfulness, thou and thy companions shall be delivered to the persecutors; and, when you shall have left what is mortal in you to be mingled with this earth, you shall come yourselves with the palm of martyrdom to rest eternally at the feet of your heavenly spouse."

Ursula felt joy and comfort in this good news; and, at dawn of day, she rose and hastened to announce it to the prelates and to her companions.

At this time the journey to Rome was attended with no ordinary difficulties, and it might well strike terror into the hearts of a legion of feeble maidens, and the apprehensions of Ursula,

THE LEGEND OF ST. URSULA.

whose pious courage was equal to the occasion, were not for herself, but for her gentle companions, and even for the prelates who counselled them, lest these might decide that it was a mere dream, suggested by the evil one to entrap them. It was, therefore, not without some feelings of misgiving that she proceeded to call them together, and told them her story, the vision of the previous night. But bishops and virgins, after listening with attention, acknowledged at once that it was the voice of God which had spoken, and that it must be obeyed. There was only one cry among the companions of the British princess, the daughter of Dionotus, " To Rome, to Rome! Let us start, in obedience to the orders of heaven!"

Ursula and her companions proceed in solemn procession to the cathedral of Cologne, where the holy viaticum is administered to them by Aquilinus, legate of Germany, who gives them all the recommendations in his power to assist them in their long journey. Thence they direct their course to the place of embarkation, escorted by the clergy and by the citizens, whether christians or pagans, for even the latter follow their footsteps with reverence. The pious widow Sigillindis, and the priest Quirillus, have joined them on their way to unite with them in

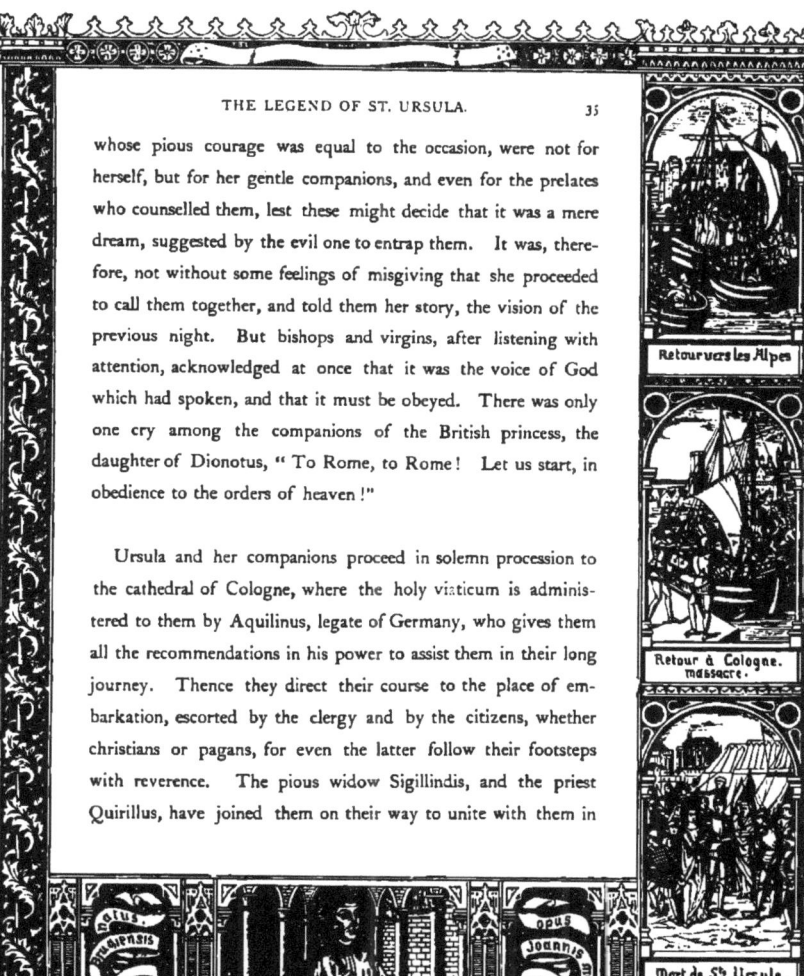

Retour vers les Alpes

Retour à Cologne.
massacre.

Mort de Ste Ursule.

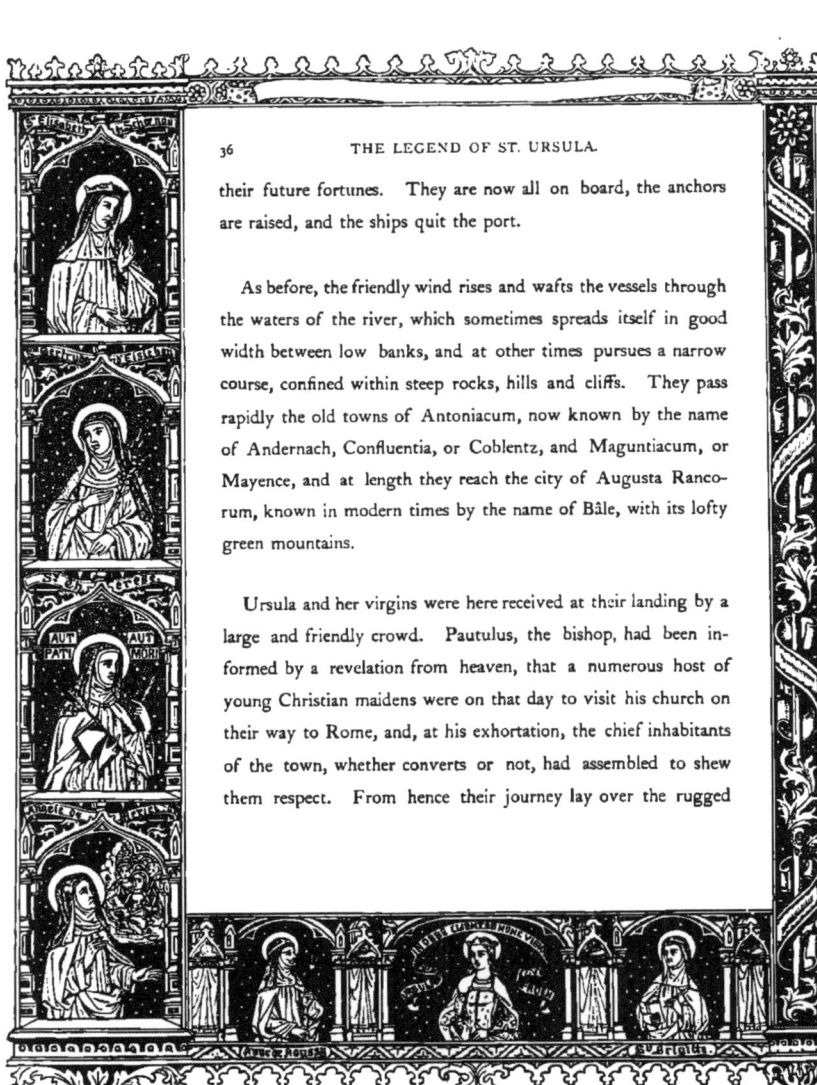

their future fortunes. They are now all on board, the anchors are raised, and the ships quit the port.

As before, the friendly wind rises and wafts the vessels through the waters of the river, which sometimes spreads itself in good width between low banks, and at other times pursues a narrow course, confined within steep rocks, hills and cliffs. They pass rapidly the old towns of Antoniacum, now known by the name of Andernach, Confluentia, or Coblentz, and Maguntiacum, or Mayence, and at length they reach the city of Augusta Rancorum, known in modern times by the name of Bâle, with its lofty green mountains.

Ursula and her virgins were here received at their landing by a large and friendly crowd. Pautulus, the bishop, had been informed by a revelation from heaven, that a numerous host of young Christian maidens were on that day to visit his church on their way to Rome, and, at his exhortation, the chief inhabitants of the town, whether converts or not, had assembled to shew them respect. From hence their journey lay over the rugged

THE LEGEND OF ST. URSULA.

Alps, and they were obliged to leave their ships and continue their pilgrimage on foot.

The preparations for departure were executed without any delay. Every arrangement was made to secure order and comfort in the march, and the legion of virgins, divided into its eleven cohorts, and each of these into subdivisions, passed out of the gates of the city, and directed their steps towards the precipitous mountains. The ships were left in the charge of Bishop Pautulus, who pronounced his blessing upon the maidens at their departure.

Three days' march brought them from the Rhine into the land of the Helvetes, and from the heights of mount Jura they descended into the vallies of the Saône and the Rhône. Both rivers were crossed, and they reached the city of Lugdunum, now called Lyons, already sanctified by its Christian martyrs, among whom the virgin Blandina was especially celebrated.

As they crossed the boundary of the province of Narbonne, the holy bishop Cæsarius, metropolitan of Gaul, himself of the

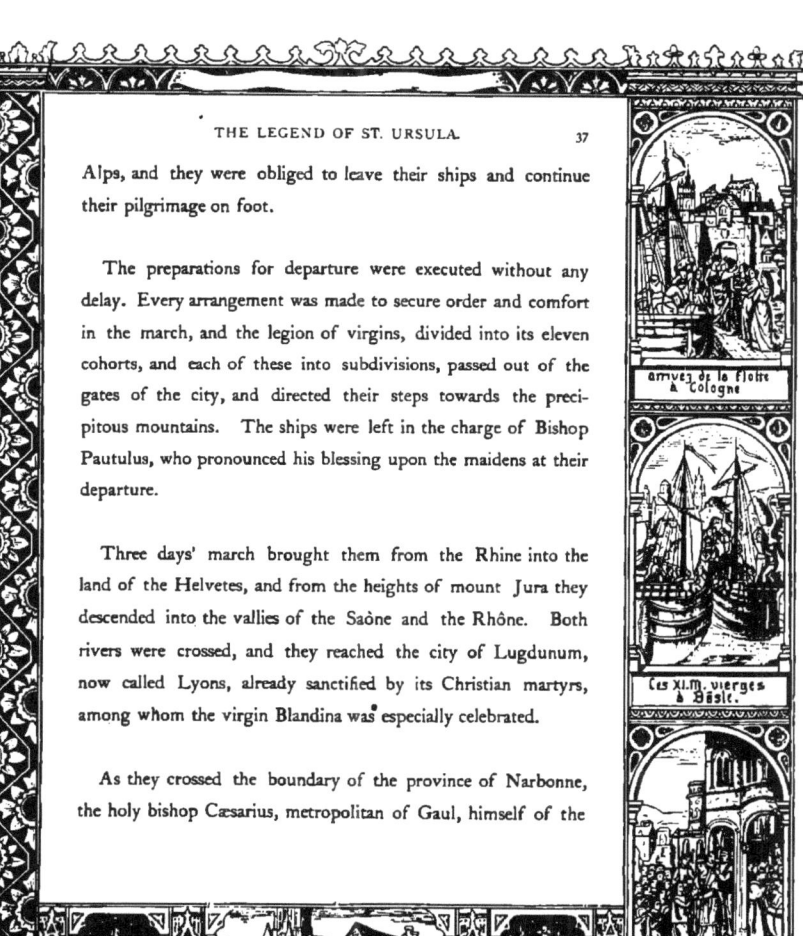

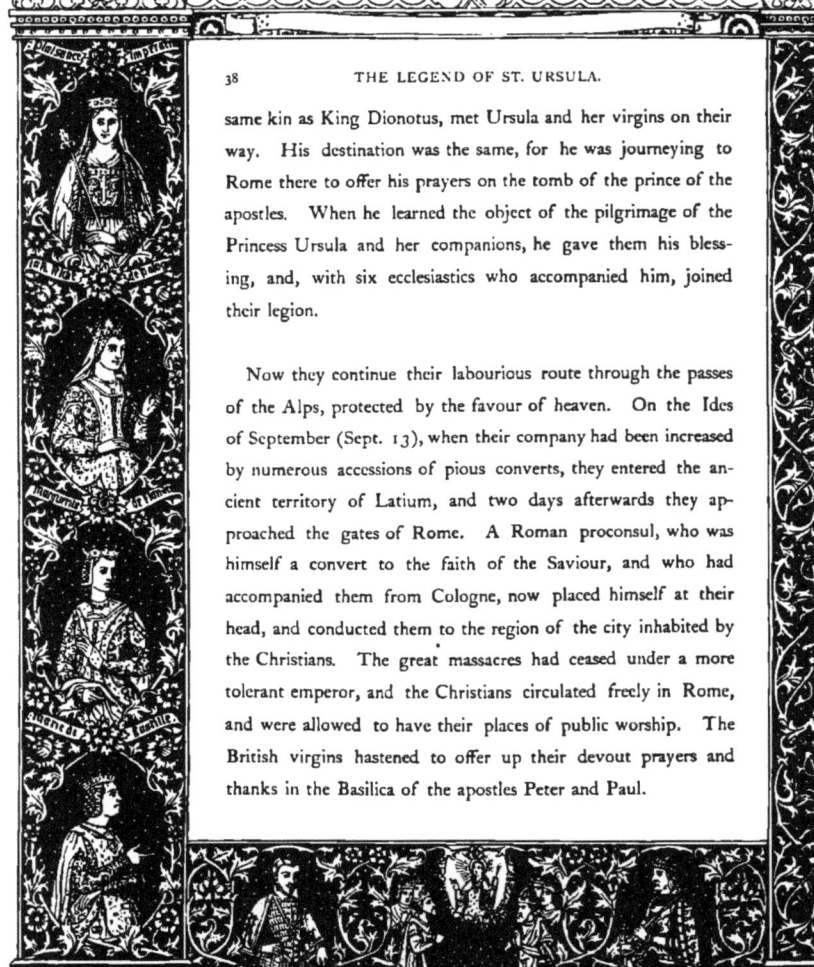

THE LEGEND OF ST. URSULA.

same kin as King Dionotus, met Ursula and her virgins on their way. His destination was the same, for he was journeying to Rome there to offer his prayers on the tomb of the prince of the apostles. When he learned the object of the pilgrimage of the Princess Ursula and her companions, he gave them his blessing, and, with six ecclesiastics who accompanied him, joined their legion.

Now they continue their labourious route through the passes of the Alps, protected by the favour of heaven. On the Ides of September (Sept. 13), when their company had been increased by numerous accessions of pious converts, they entered the ancient territory of Latium, and two days afterwards they approached the gates of Rome. A Roman proconsul, who was himself a convert to the faith of the Saviour, and who had accompanied them from Cologne, now placed himself at their head, and conducted them to the region of the city inhabited by the Christians. The great massacres had ceased under a more tolerant emperor, and the Christians circulated freely in Rome, and were allowed to have their places of public worship. The British virgins hastened to offer up their devout prayers and thanks in the Basilica of the apostles Peter and Paul.

THE LEGEND OF ST. URSULA.

The pope who had already received information of the arrival of these new visitors, and had dressed himself in the pontifical robes, with the tiara on his head, and cross at his side, entered the sacred temple to receive them. At his view, they all fell down before him, and venerated the successor of St. Peter, the representative of the divine majesty on earth. Space was wanting to admit all the members of this numerous cortege, and many were obliged to be satisfied with contemplating the supreme pontiff from a distance, and with testifying their joy by their emotion. But in front of them all knelt the Princess Ursula, calm in countenance, and attentive to the words of the pontiff, with her hands joined and eyes directed to heaven. The pope invoked the blessing of heaven upon them all, and, touched with the noble bearing and piety of the young princess, addressed her in words of encouragement, exhorting her to continue always in the same course which she had so worthily begun.

The Christians of Rome received the British virgins with joy, and lavished upon them every hospitable attention in their power. Roman matrons, and senators and knights, watched over their safety and over their comforts. They passed the days in visiting the relics and holy places under the guidance of the supreme

THE LEGEND OF ST. URSULA.

pontiff himself, and especially they all offered up their vows at the shrine of St. Peter.

It must not be supposed that all the eleven thousand virgins who left Britain were baptized Christians. Gathered together from the numerous petty kingdoms into which the island was divided, most of which remained still buried in the darkness of paganism, they had all, during their three years' noviciate, been instructed in the truths of the Christian faith, but many of them had been reserved to receive the sacrament of baptism from worthier hands than could be found at home. The pope, whom the legend names Cyriac, prepared to perform this imposing ceremony in his own person.

On the day fixed for the baptismal rite, Cyriac caused to be displayed all the pomp and splendour of his religion. The catechumens, clothed in white tunics, carrying torches in their hands, and surrounded by their brothers and sisters in faith, proceeded from their residence to the baptistery built near the basilica of St. Peter *in Monte*, a monument of primitive simplicity, resembling more a tomb than a church, but for the light which entered it from a few small windows, which was in-

creased a little by the glare of the tapers. The men had already been baptized in the first inclosure of the edifice, when the supreme pontiff proceeded into the interior to perform the same ceremony on the virgins. There stood several large fonts of marble destined for this sacred performance. There two of the virgins, named in the legend Lucia and Anastasia, relatives of Conan the betrothed of Ursula, followed by their companions, having prepared themselves for the holy ceremony according to the rules established in the church, immersed themselves in water. Cyriac, clothed in a white tunic, and followed by the holy college and his clergy and deacons then entered. The venerable pontiff addressed to the virgins some last words of instruction, and then proceeded to give them that new birth which made them full members of the church of Christ. Ursula, standing near her companions, rejoiced in their happiness, and listened with respect to the words of God as they issued from the lips of the pontiff.

The ceremony being finished, the holy band employed their time in visiting the tombs of those who had fallen asleep in Jesus, and whose remains were laid in the different churches of the heaven-favoured city. Some of the heathen populace fol-

THE LEGEND OF ST. URSULA.

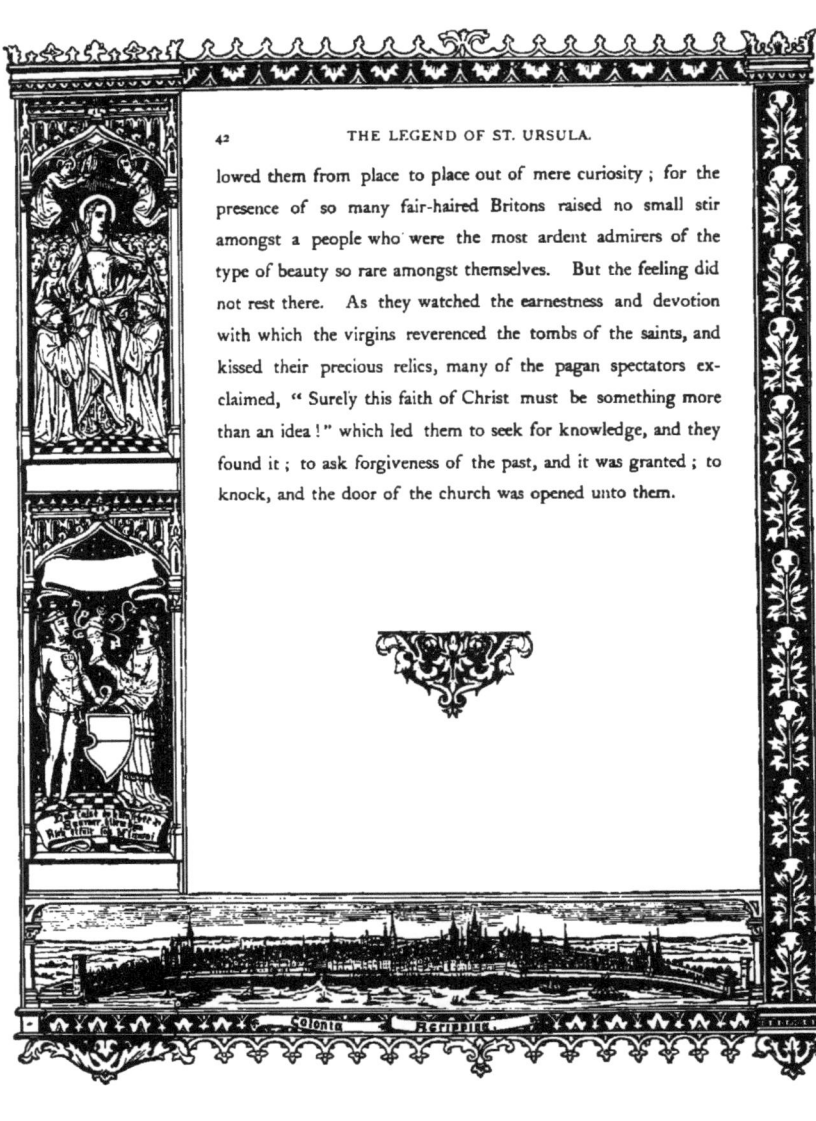

lowed them from place to place out of mere curiosity; for the presence of so many fair-haired Britons raised no small stir amongst a people who were the most ardent admirers of the type of beauty so rare amongst themselves. But the feeling did not rest there. As they watched the earnestness and devotion with which the virgins reverenced the tombs of the saints, and kissed their precious relics, many of the pagan spectators exclaimed, " Surely this faith of Christ must be something more than an idea!" which led them to seek for knowledge, and they found it; to ask forgiveness of the past, and it was granted; to knock, and the door of the church was opened unto them.

CHAPTER VI.

URSULA AND HER COMPANIONS LEAVE ROME;—BALE;—
MAYENCE;—MEETING OF URSULA AND CONAN.

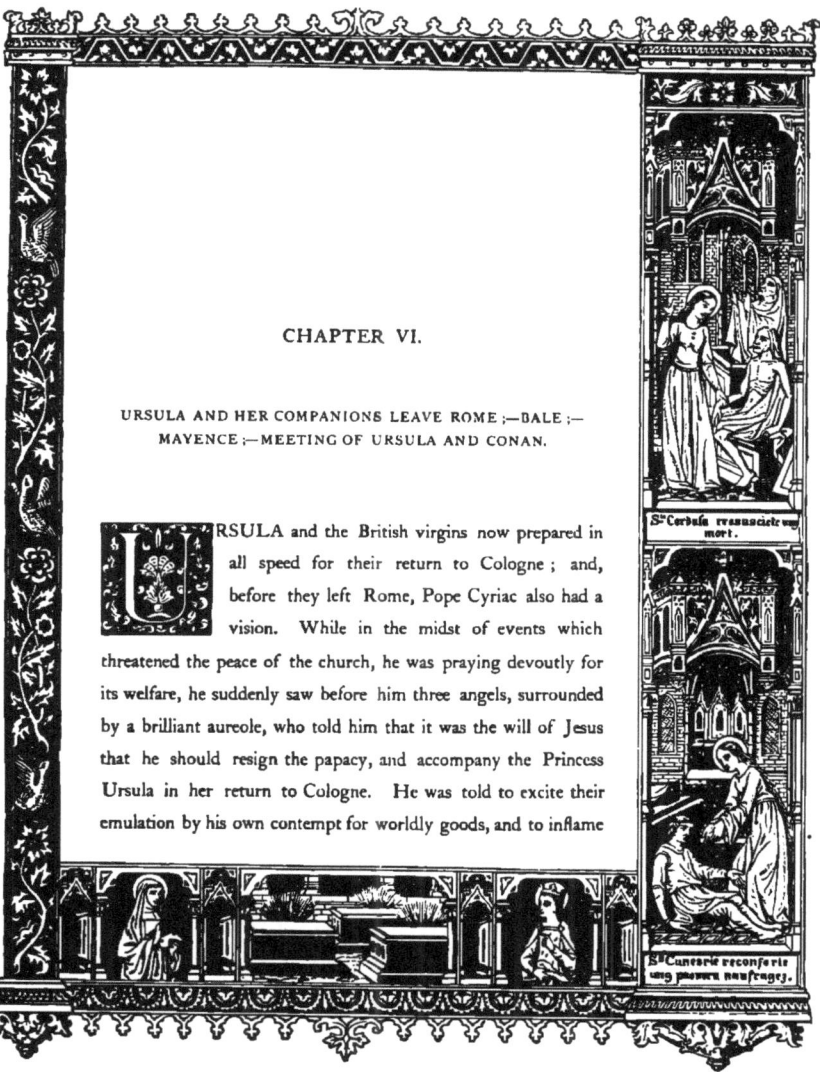

St Cordula ressuscietè un mort.

St Cunerie reconforte ung pauvres naufragez.

URSULA and the British virgins now prepared in all speed for their return to Cologne; and, before they left Rome, Pope Cyriac also had a vision. While in the midst of events which threatened the peace of the church, he was praying devoutly for its welfare, he suddenly saw before him three angels, surrounded by a brilliant aureole, who told him that it was the will of Jesus that he should resign the papacy, and accompany the Princess Ursula in her return to Cologne. He was told to excite their emulation by his own contempt for worldly goods, and to inflame

44   THE LEGEND OF ST. URSULA.

their courage by his eloquence and the purity of his actions. His reward was to be the same martyrdom with which the virgin pilgrims were soon to be crowned.

Cyriac weighed deeply in his mind the admonitions of the angels, and for several days he remained silent on the revelation with which he had been favoured; but, when the day fixed for Ursula's departure arrived, he called together his ministers, and told them of his vision, and informed them of his fixed resolution to obey the will of heaven. They expostulated earnestly, but in vain. Several bishops and princes of the church, with some of the noblest of the Roman citizens, touched by the devotion of their pontiff, followed his example, and resolved upon joining in the march to Cologne.

With so many additions, the legion had to form in a somewhat different order in its return to that which had been observed in its march to Rome. The virgins took the lead; after them came the matrons and the children; and then the bishops, with the Pontiff Cyriac at their head. These latter formed a camp apart; on Sundays and saints' days only, at the time of halting, they introduced themselves into the ranks of the legion to per-

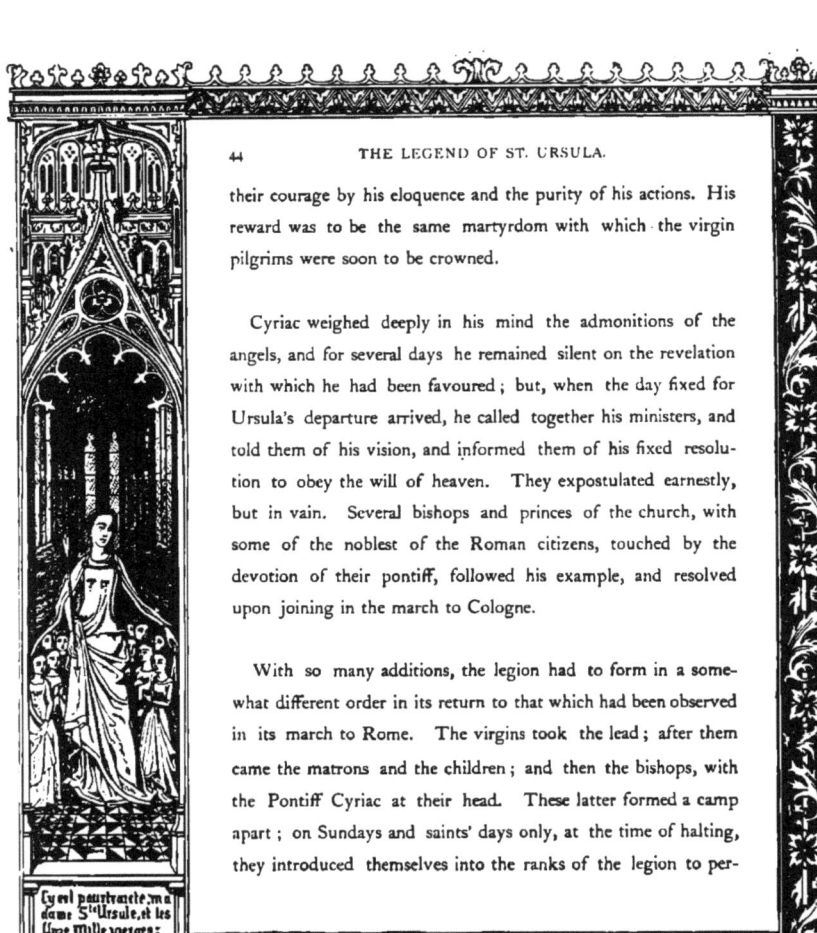

THE LEGEND OF ST. URSULA.

form the duties of their sacred office. The kings, princes, and knights, closed the march.

In this order, they proceeded for the last time to kneel before the tomb of the apostles, and then they marched out of Rome, through an immense crowd of spectators.

It was the close of the month of September. In a few days they had passed through Latium, Etouria, and Liguria, and found themselves again threading the passages of the Alps. Heaven favoured them on their march, and without meeting with any untoward event, they again saw before them the Augusta Rancorum—the city of Bâle, where Ursula had left her ships.

A holy hermit, who had his cell in a nook in the mountain, saw the approach of the legion of virgins as it emerged from a pass, and hastened to the city to inform the ministers of the church ; and the whole body of the clergy hurried to the gate of the town to await their arrival. They had not to wait long ; and as Pope Cyriac and Ursula, who walked side by side at the head of the march, approached, priests and monks fell on their

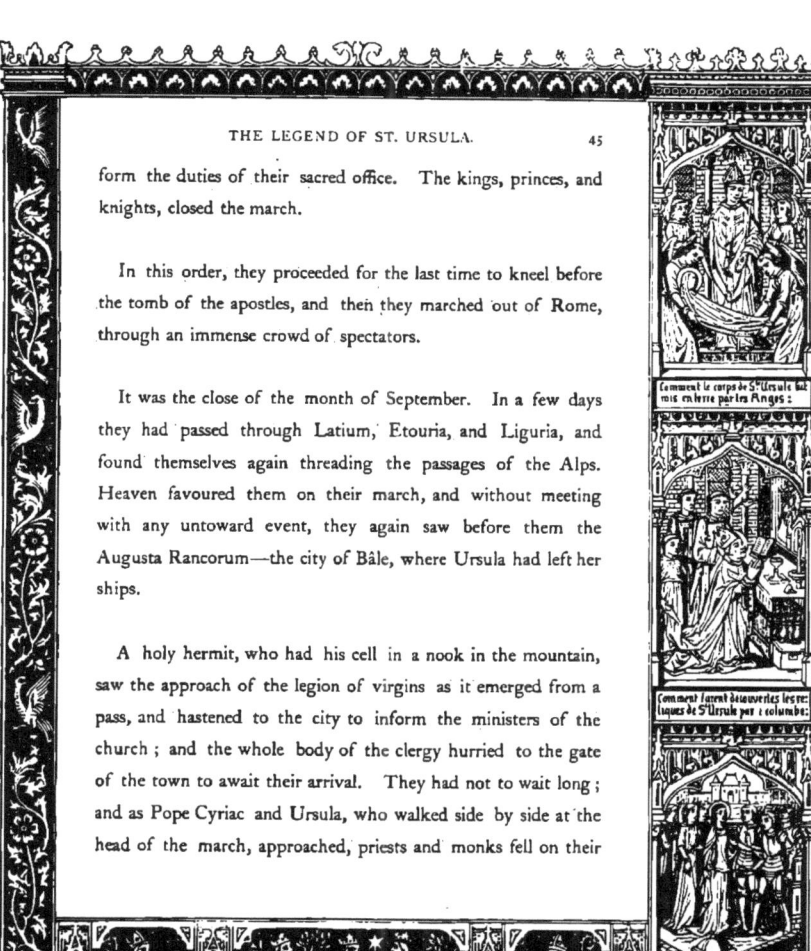

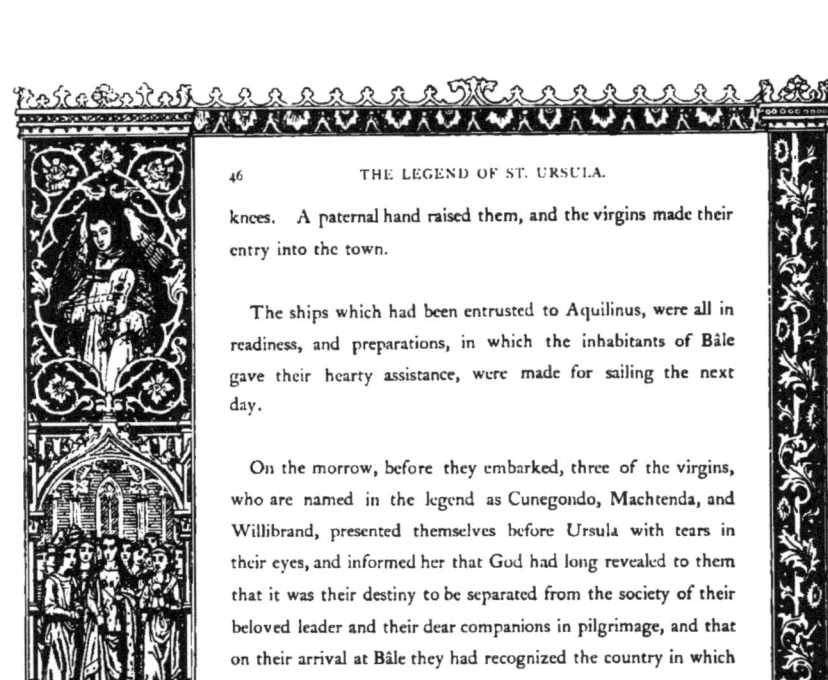

knees. A paternal hand raised them, and the virgins made their entry into the town.

The ships which had been entrusted to Aquilinus, were all in readiness, and preparations, in which the inhabitants of Bâle gave their hearty assistance, were made for sailing the next day.

On the morrow, before they embarked, three of the virgins, who are named in the legend as Cunegondo, Machtenda, and Willibrand, presented themselves before Ursula with tears in their eyes, and informed her that God had long revealed to them that it was their destiny to be separated from the society of their beloved leader and their dear companions in pilgrimage, and that on their arrival at Bâle they had recognized the country in which they were to remain. They had that day again felt the heavenly warning in their hearts, and they had come to bid her adieu. Their grief at parting was somewhat lessened by the knowledge that they were soon to join her in martyrdom.

While the Princess Ursula was thus on her way back to Cologne, a prince from the isle of Britain, in whose fate she

THE LEGEND OF ST URSULA.

was especially interested, was approaching to meet her. Three years had now nearly expired since Ursula had left her country, and during that time several events of importance had occurred. Agrippinus, king of the Picts, had died, after himself accepting the Christian faith. Conan, who succeeded him on the throne, had become a sincere convert, and his mother, the Queen Demetria, had also been gathered within the fold of Christ.

During the long period of Ursula's absence Conan had never ceased to bewail her loss. The time had now arrived when, by the solemn contract made between them, they should be united. Still there were no news of the absent ones. Day after day Conan would repair to the coast, and eagerly scan the horizon, in order to catch the first glimpse of the long-expected fleet. The nobles, too, whose daughters had accompanied Ursula on her voyage, were eager in their enquiries after the holy band. Suspense at length became intolerable, and Conan determined that, by the help of God assisting him, he would fit out a vessel and sail in quest of her whom he so tenderly loved. This project he carried immediately into execution, and about the beginning of September, in the year 237, he set sail from the coast of Albion,

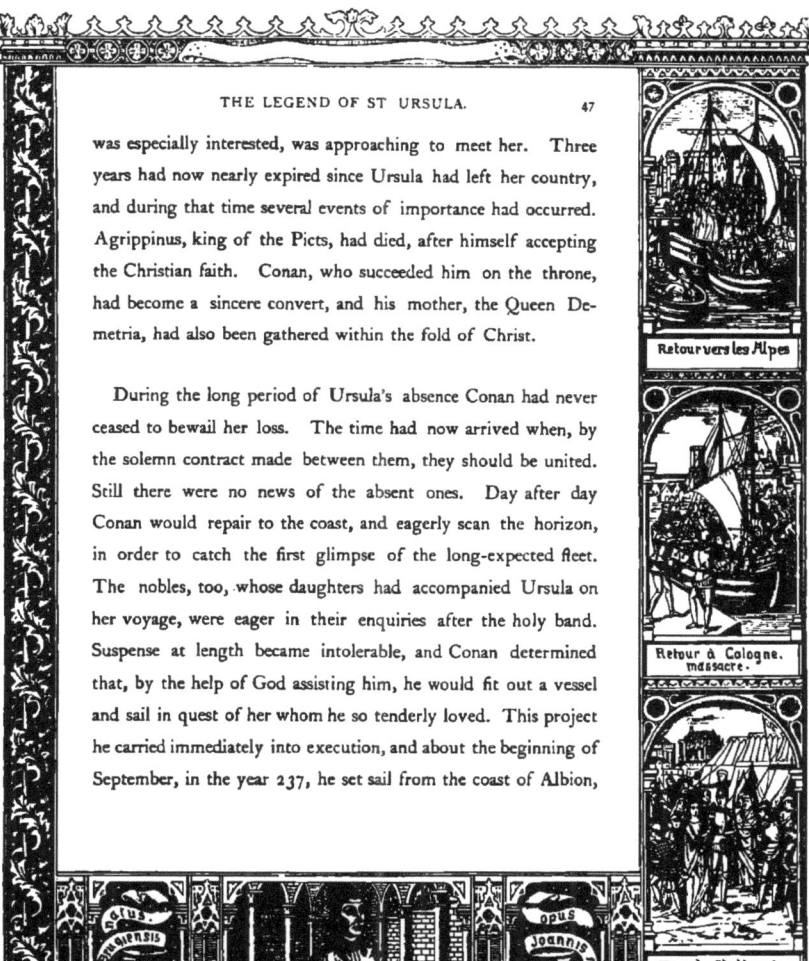

Retour vers les Alpes

Retour à Cologne. massacre.

Mort de Ste Ursule.

THE LEGEND OF ST. URSULA

accompanied by Demetria, his mother, his sister Florentine, and several princes and nobles of his court.

Conan does not appear to have received any intimation where his affianced bride then was, or even of the direction she had taken after leaving her native country. He therefore resigned himself entirely to the guidance of providence, feeling that if the course he had undertaken was agreeable to the divine will, Heaven itself would direct him in his journey. With implicit faith, therefore, he pursued his way, not doubting that he would arrive at the object of his search. Nor was his confidence misplaced: for he had no sooner lost sight of the shores of Britain than a gentle westerly wind safely wafted his vessel to the mouth of the Rhine. He proceeded up the river without making any stoppage until he arrived at the city of Maguntiacum, now called Mayence.

Rutherius was at that time Bishop of Maguntiacum, and an earnest disciple of Christ. As soon as he heard of the arrival of the British prince, he gathered together the principal of his clergy, and at their head marched in solemn procession to the

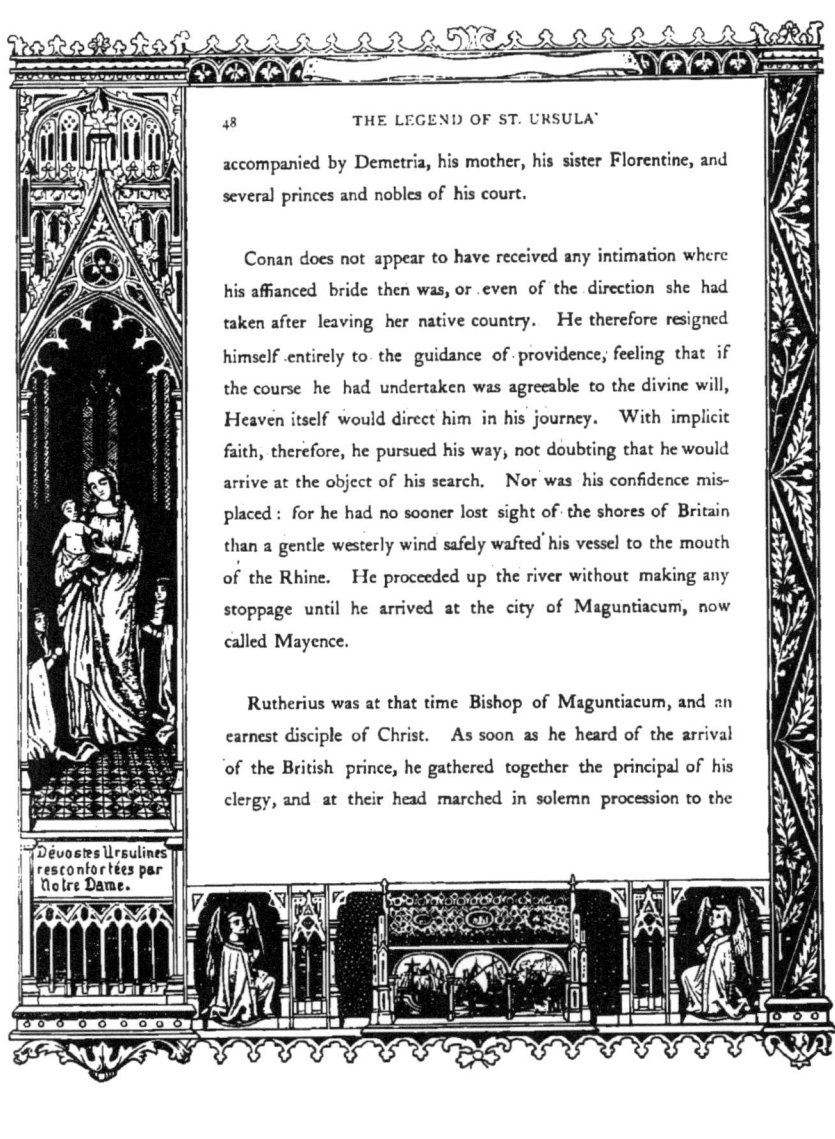

Dévostes Ursulines resconfortées par Notre Dame.

THE LEGEND OF ST. URSULA.

port in order to receive him with all the respect due to his exalted position. Although Conan had not as yet openly professed the Christian faith, he regarded the holy bishop, who was awaiting him on the shore with the most profound veneration, and throwing himself on his knees before him, inquired whether Rutherius could give him any tidings of the virgin Ursula. The holy man, well knowing by divine inspiration that Conan was a chosen vessel in the hands of the Lord, was moved with compassion at the solicitude he displayed towards the Christian princess. Raising him from the ground, and tenderly embracing him, he said,—

"Be not too solicitous, my son, about the affairs of this world. She whom you seek is now at Rome, but you shall shortly see her. Be content to await her arrival in this city; and, in order to render yourself more worthy of her, let me entreat you to embrace that faith which is her only joy and consolation."

Conan was much moved by the tender solicitude expressed by Rutherius, and promised to remain in Maguntiacum until the object of his dearest affections should arrive. Meanwhile the

THE LEGEND OF ST. URSULA.

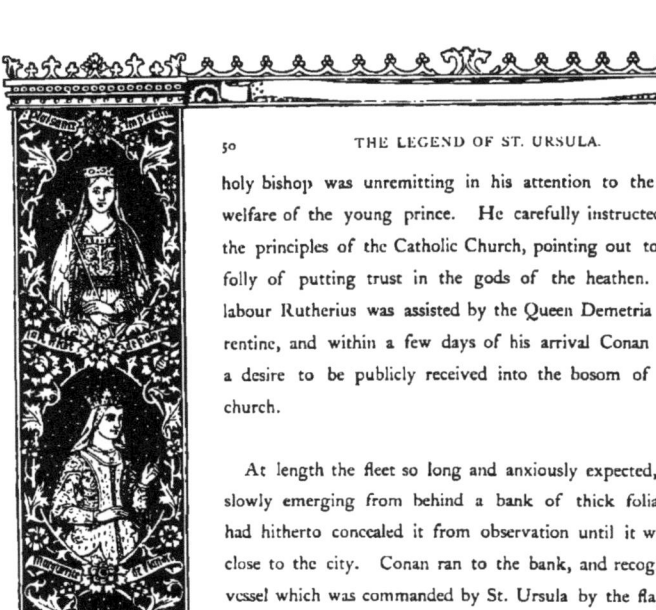

holy bishop was unremitting in his attention to the spiritual welfare of the young prince. He carefully instructed him in the principles of the Catholic Church, pointing out to him the folly of putting trust in the gods of the heathen. In this labour Rutherius was assisted by the Queen Demetria and Florentine, and within a few days of his arrival Conan expressed a desire to be publicly received into the bosom of the holy church.

At length the fleet so long and anxiously expected, appeared slowly emerging from behind a bank of thick foliage which had hitherto concealed it from observation until it was arrived close to the city. Conan ran to the bank, and recognizing the vessel which was commanded by St. Ursula by the flag charged with ermine which floated gracefully from the mast, stood ready to welcome his betrothed as soon as she disembarked. With the dignity of a queen, blended with the humility of a saint, the virgin received his salutations. The Bishops Cyriacus and Rutherius were much moved on witnessing the meeting of the noble pair—never more to be separated on earth, and shortly to be co-partners in everlasting glory—and invoking a blessing upon them, prayed that they might be endued with strength

THE LEGEND OF ST. URSULA.

to bear the trials they were soon to undergo. The ecclesiastics and the holy virgins then formed a procession and walked to the cathedral to render thanks to God for his goodness and mercy in thus bringing them together again after passing through so many difficulties and dangers.

After the public acknowledgment of divine favour had been solemnly rendered, Conan, accompanied by all the principal of the clergy, St. Ursula, Demetria his mother, and his sister Florentine, withdrew into the baptistry, where he received from the hands of Cyriacus the solemn sacrament of baptism. The ceremony was performed according to the custom practised in the primitive church; that is, Conan was totally immersed in the piscina or font which contained the holy water. Many of the followers of the prince at the same time imitated the example of their august master, and a great number of neophytes were that day added to the fold of Christ. The following day it became known by divine revelation that in three days the blood of the holy martyrs should be poured out in Cologne; notwithstanding which the utmost joy and serenity prevailed amongst them, and all seemed anxious to reach the place where they were to lay down their lives for the cause of Christ. Imi-

THE LEGEND OF ST. URSULA.

tating the example of St. Ursula, the virgins stripped themselves of all their jewels and other valuables, which they distributed to the poor. They then hastened to the port, and embarked on their vessels which were to bear them to the scene of their martyrdom. The whole city flocked to the banks to take their leave of the blessed legion. The sobbings and tears of those on shore were responded to with words of prayer and praise, while above the confused murmur of lamentation and the monotonous plash of the oars, as with measured beat they sank into the water, might be heard the voice of Cyriacus, clear and firm, urging his weaker companions to remain steadfast, and with fervid eloquence calling on them to remember that a double crown was laid up for them in Heaven — the crown of virginity and the crown of martyrdom.

Rutherius, with the clergy and people, remained by the river until the last notes of Vespers feebly reached them from the boats, now far on their journey. With heavy hearts they slowly returned to the cathedral church, where fervent prayers were offered for the devoted saints, that the grace of Jesus Christ might sustain them throughout their awful trial. A feeling of

Tombeau de S.-Ursule à Cologne.

desolation oppressed their spirits akin to that which filled the hearts of the disciples of Jesus when on Calvary's mount the agonizing cry, "It is finished!" escaped from His sacred lips. But they sorrowed not as men without hope, for they were well assured that legions of angels were earnestly longing to bear their sanctified souls to everlasting rest, and that the Adorable Son Himself waited to receive them.

Already did the devout Christians of Maguntiacum regard the blessed virgins as martyrs, and esteem as priceless treasures the jewels and other articles which they had bestowed upon the Church for the benefit of the poor. Happy, thrice happy, are those blessed spots wherein are yet preserved the relics of the saints. With what holy joy does the devout pilgrim visit the city where repose the tangible remembrances of some sainted disciple of our Lord! Who can contemplate without feelings of emotion the tomb of a blessed martyr? or whose heart does not burn within him as his foot presses the soil once reddened with the blood of those who, refusing to deny their master, remained faithful to the death?

Rutherius, and others of his clergy, remained prostrate before

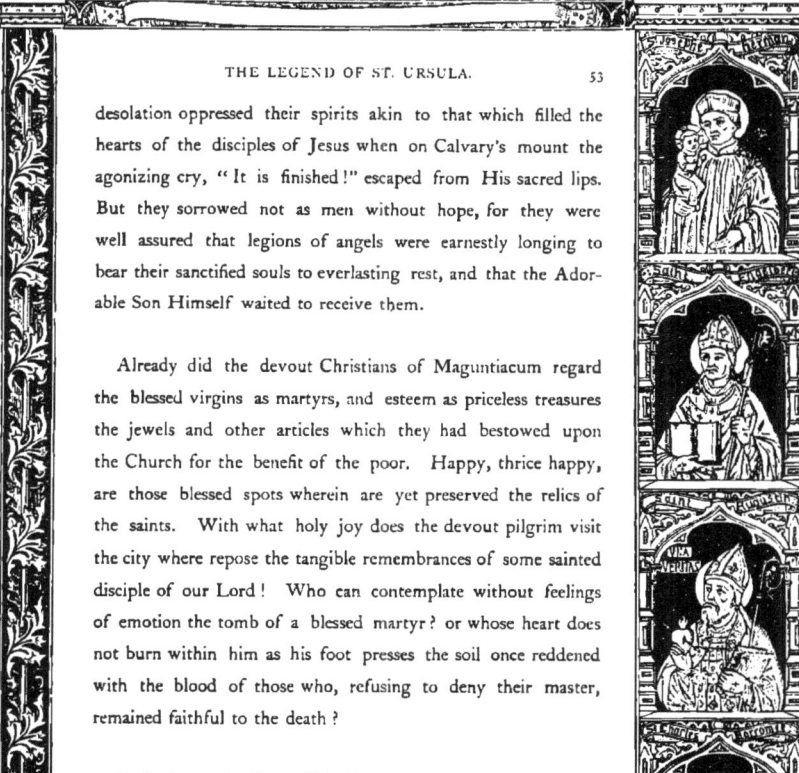

THE LEGEND OF ST. URSULA.

the altar of the church throughout the night; nor were their prayers offered in vain: for the bodies and souls of the virgins were miraculously strengthened, so that they sped onwards with alacrity, assured that every hour their happiness was approaching fruition. So ready—nay, so desirous—were they of laying down their lives for the glory of their blessed Saviour, that in places where the broadened river ran sluggishly on its course, the occupants of each boat toiled with unwearied efforts to hasten their progress—jealous lest another should be the first to reach the wished-for port. And thus they journeyed onwards.

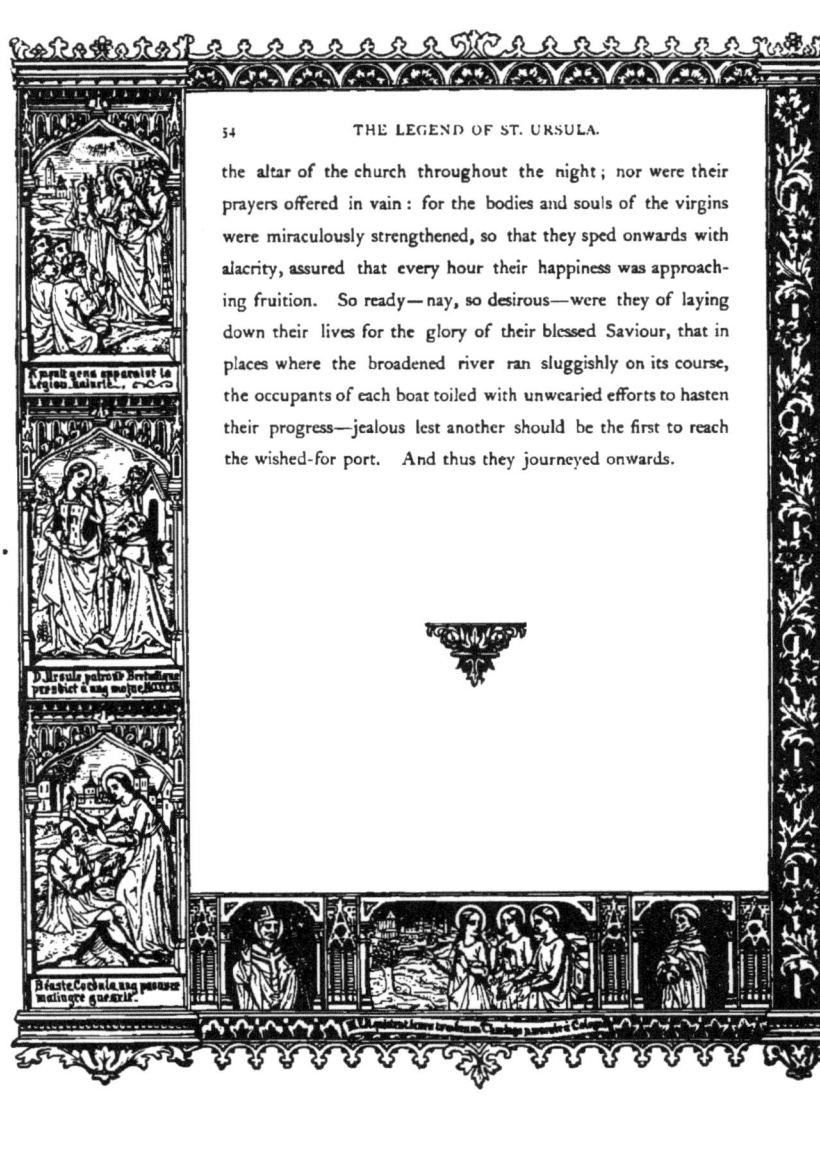

CHAPTER VII.

ST. URSULA PROCEEDS TO COLOGNE.—THE MASSACRE.

A T THIS time the Roman empire was ruled by the Emperor Alexander Severus, and he had marched to the banks of the Rhine with an army, not only to check the invasions of the barbarians on the frontier of the empire, but to suppress rebellion among the imperial legions, which also were composed in a great degree of barbarians. One night, while he was reposing in his tent, his guard was suddenly overpowered and massacred by a horde of Huns, who burst into the tent and slew the emperor. The assassins were in the pay of the traitor Maximinus, who secretly

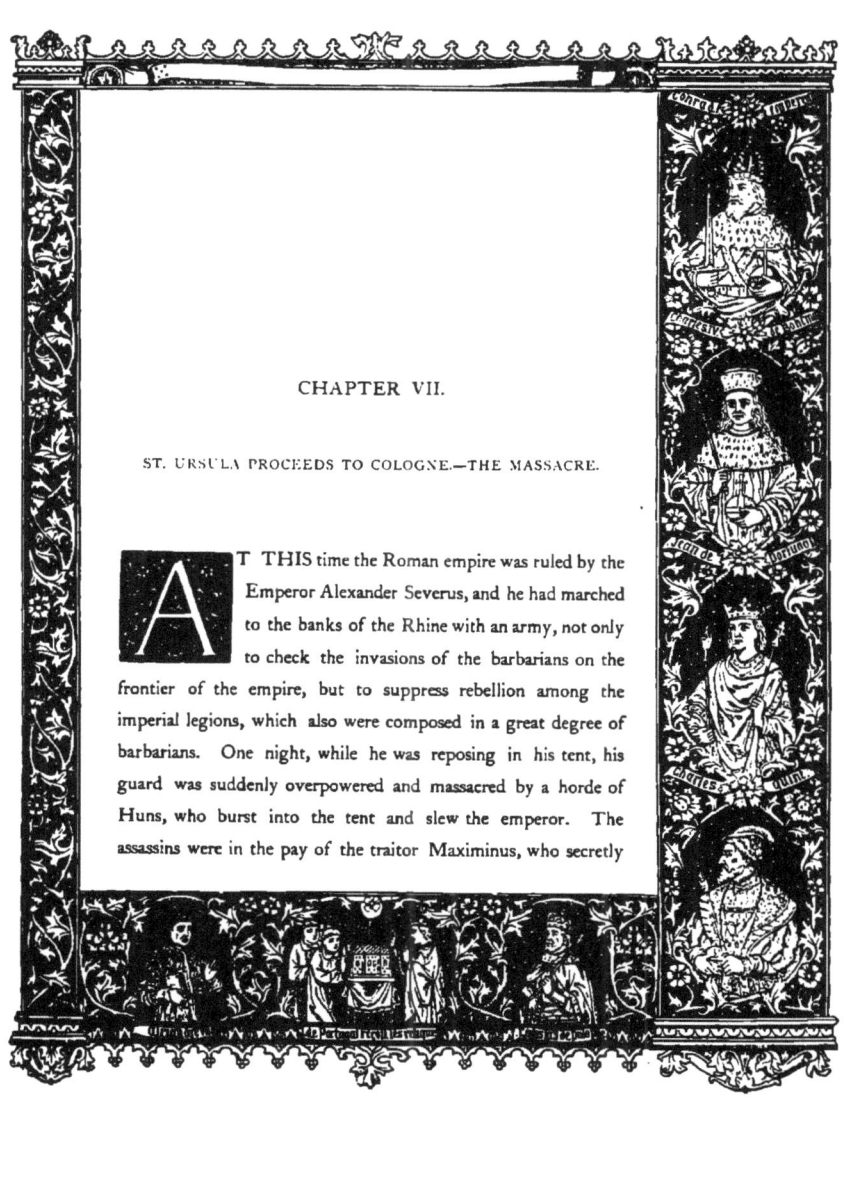

THE LEGEND OF ST. URSULA.

aspired to the empire. The latter had no sooner assured himself of the success of his plot, than he addressed hypocritically the legions who remained faithful, and urged them to take vengeance for the murder of the emperor, and they fell upon the Huns who had perpetrated the crime, and slew them all. Maximinus now caused himself to be proclaimed emperor by his troops, and succeeded by his boldness and cunning in reducing to obedience the legions which had revolted. One of the first acts of the new emperor was to publish an edict against the Christians, of whom he was a well-known persecutor.

The savage Huns lay encamped in the plains of Cologne at the time when Ursula and her companions were sailing down the Rhine. They passed Confluentia, or Coblentz, and glided peacefully under the rocks of Ehrenbreitstein, and on the following morning, which was the 21st of October, 237, the blessed company of saints approached the city of Cologne. Joy and gladness reigned in their hearts at the prospect of their speedy glorification, and the air resounded with hymns of praise. The fields on the banks of the river were bare: the generous earth had just yielded her fruit of golden grain and purple grapes, and now another harvest was about to be gathered in—a harvest

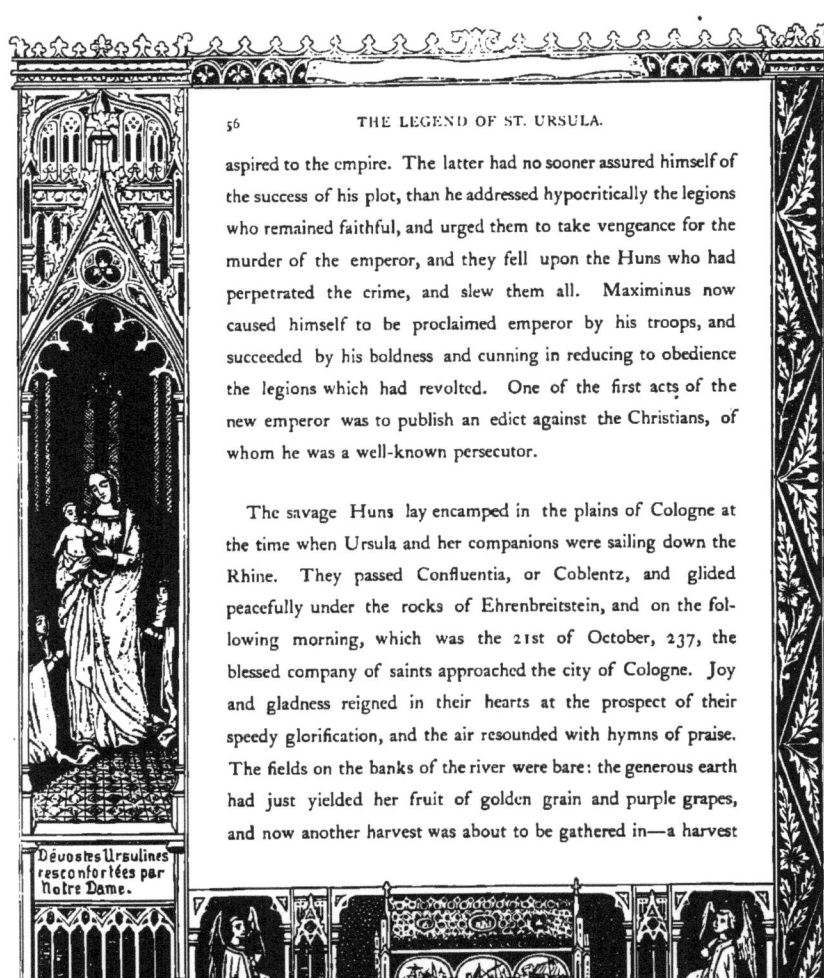

Dévostes Ursulines resconfortées par Notre Dame.

THE LEGEND OF ST. URSULA. 57

of blessed martyrs to be treasured in the garner above. As the little fleet was calmly wafted down the river, ineffable peace and serenity filled every heart, and every tongue gave utterance to sentiments of fervid adoration.

Then the holy Bishop Cyriacus, his soul melting with love for his adorable Saviour, and earnestly longing to be with Him, wearing the glorious crown of martyrdom, thus addressed his companions :—

"But a short time longer, my dear children, and your enemies, who are now waiting as wolves to destroy the flock of Christ, shall be themselves the instruments of your glory. Let us teach them, by our readiness to meet death, that our hopes are placed beyond the world. Remember, my children, the words of our Blessed Lord. He it is who has promised to give unto them, who fight the good fight, an everlasting crown : and that to which he has plighted his word He will faithfully perform."

When at dawn of day the Huns perceived the boats approaching the city, they rushed to the banks of the river to learn who

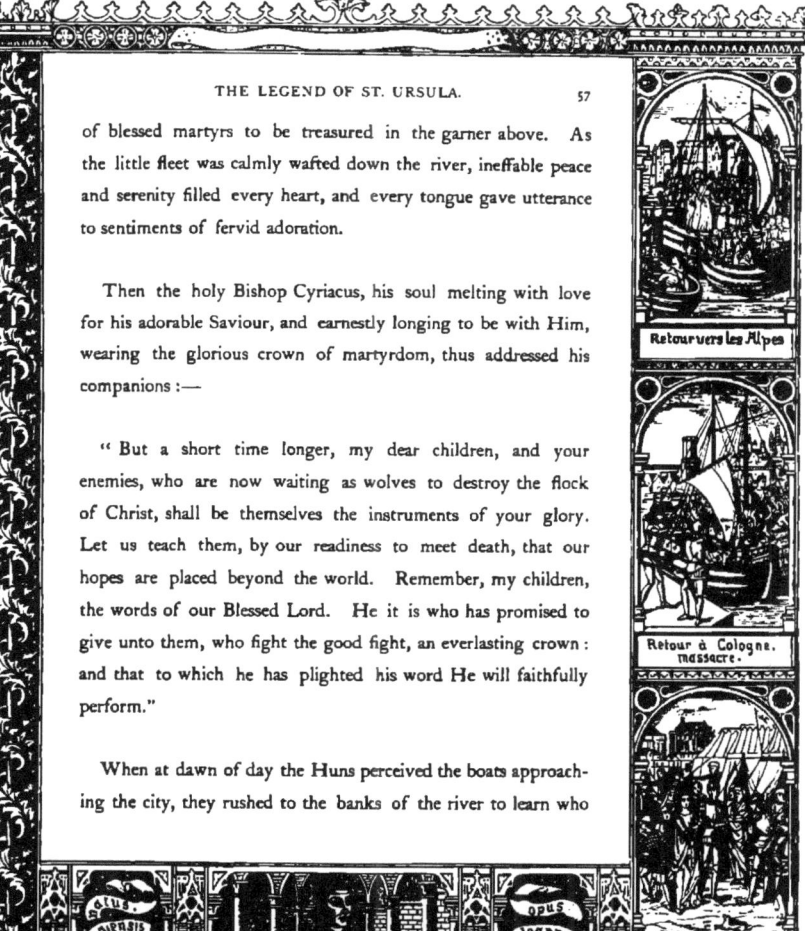

Retour vers les Alpes

Retour à Cologne.
massacre.

Mort de Ste Ursule.

THE LEGEND OF ST. URSULA.

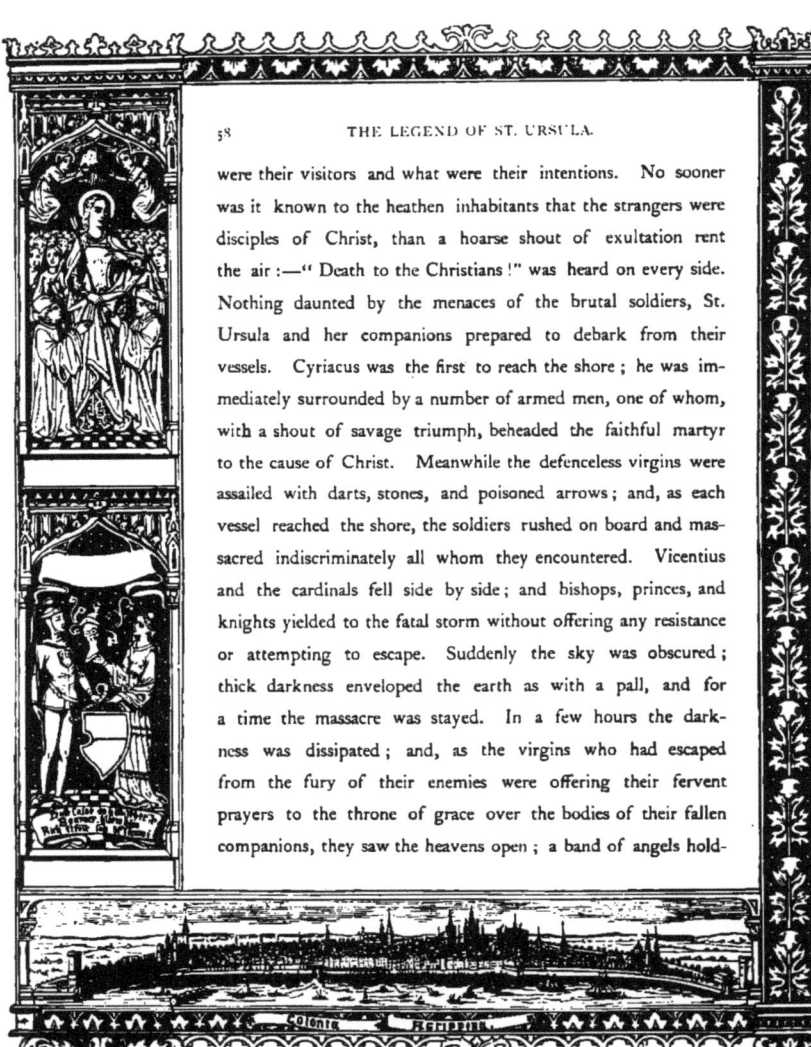

were their visitors and what were their intentions. No sooner was it known to the heathen inhabitants that the strangers were disciples of Christ, than a hoarse shout of exultation rent the air :—" Death to the Christians !" was heard on every side. Nothing daunted by the menaces of the brutal soldiers, St. Ursula and her companions prepared to debark from their vessels. Cyriacus was the first to reach the shore ; he was immediately surrounded by a number of armed men, one of whom, with a shout of savage triumph, beheaded the faithful martyr to the cause of Christ. Meanwhile the defenceless virgins were assailed with darts, stones, and poisoned arrows ; and, as each vessel reached the shore, the soldiers rushed on board and massacred indiscriminately all whom they encountered. Vicentius and the cardinals fell side by side ; and bishops, princes, and knights yielded to the fatal storm without offering any resistance or attempting to escape. Suddenly the sky was obscured ; thick darkness enveloped the earth as with a pall, and for a time the massacre was stayed. In a few hours the darkness was dissipated ; and, as the virgins who had escaped from the fury of their enemies were offering their fervent prayers to the throne of grace over the bodies of their fallen companions, they saw the heavens open ; a band of angels hold-

THE LEGEND OF ST. URSULA.

ing palms towards them, encouraged them to remain faithful to the death, pointing out to them those of their associates who had already gained their crowns of martyrdom, seated on thrones around the Lamb. For a time the barbarians were awe-stricken at the constancy of the devoted band; but, instigated by their leaders, they recommenced their fiendish work. Rightly conjecturing, Ursula and Conan, her betrothed—who, since his baptism, had taken the name of Ætherius—to be in command of the holy company, the soldiers dragged them to the tent of Aasvahs, the chief of the Huns. No sooner did his eyes fall upon the angelic face and form of the young virgin, than he was completely dazzled by her transcendant beauty, and determined that she should not be sacrificed with the others. Ætherius, he sentenced to instant execution, fearing him as a rival as much as he hated him as a Christian.

For one moment, when Ursula heard the fatal mandate, her eyes, eloquent with love, fell upon Ætherius, as though she would intercede for his life; but the grace of God never forsook her, and no earthly feeling was allowed to exert its sway. As the executioner rudely laid his mailed hand upon Ætherius to lead him to his death, the young Christian hesitated to be torn

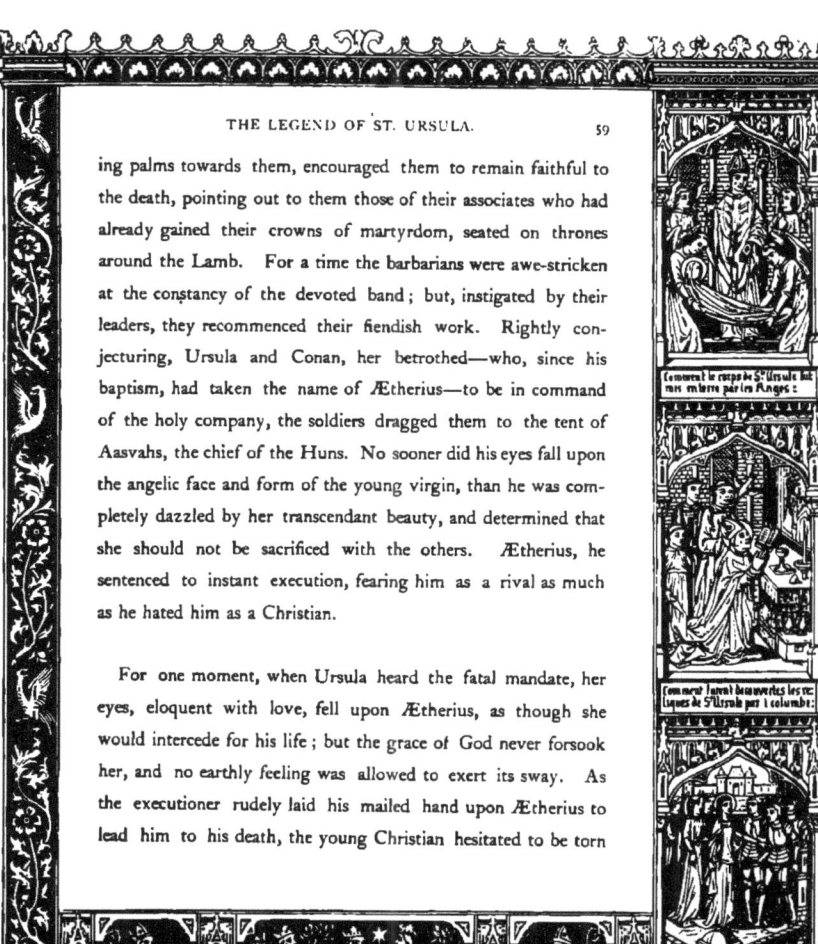

from the side of her whom he loved; but one glance from St. Ursula, beaming with superhuman light, assured him, and he quietly resigned himself into the hands of his murderers. A few paces only from where the sainted virgin was standing, a soldier armed with a sword struck the head of Ætherius to the earth, while his blessed spirit hastened to its everlasting abode, there shortly to meet her whom he loved so tenderly on earth.

Having removed this obstacle from his path, Aasvahs urged his suit with all the dissimulation of which he was master. He represented to St. Ursula the advantages which she would enjoy were she united to him; and even went so far as to assure her that in that exalted position she would be able to render great services in the propagation of the faith she professed. He could not believe that herself, the daughter of a prince, would form an alliance with any one below her own station; and here was the illustrious chief of the victorious Huns, before whom Rome herself trembled, who laid his conquests and his love at her feet. To this appeal Ursula remained silent. With downcast eyes, and hands devoutly pressed together, she was earnestly praying for help from above to deliver her from the snares in which the evil one was endeavouring to entangle her. This silence was interpreted by the heathen tyrant to signify her assent to his proposal; and, kneeling before her, he saluted her as Queen of the Huns. "Hail, Queen of the Huns!" shouted the attendant lords; the cry was caught up by the barbarian horde, and "Hail, Queen of the Huns!" was echoed from a thousand throats.

Motionless as a statue, radiant as a beautiful vision, St. Ursula stood before the arrogant barbarian. The salutations of the lords, and the hoarse shouts of the multitude alike unmoved her. Was it possible that she was about to yield to the evil whisperings of the great enemy of souls now that immortal life and happiness were actually dawning upon her, and Heaven's gates thrown wide open to receive her soul within their glorious portals? Who shall say what agonizing temptations were permitted to assail her at that moment? If Christ our Saviour—incapable of sin—was not exempt from the machinations of Satan, it is not too presumptuous on our part to imagine that the constancy of the sainted virgin was similarly proved. As Queen of the Huns she would have it in her power to further the cause of Christ by protecting its professors: nay, could she

62 THE LEGEND OF ST. URSULA.

not save the lives of those of her companions who had so far escaped the massacre? On the one hand there were dignity, honour, wealth—on the other a cruel death, but consequent upon this death was everlasting life.

St. Ursula resolved which to choose.

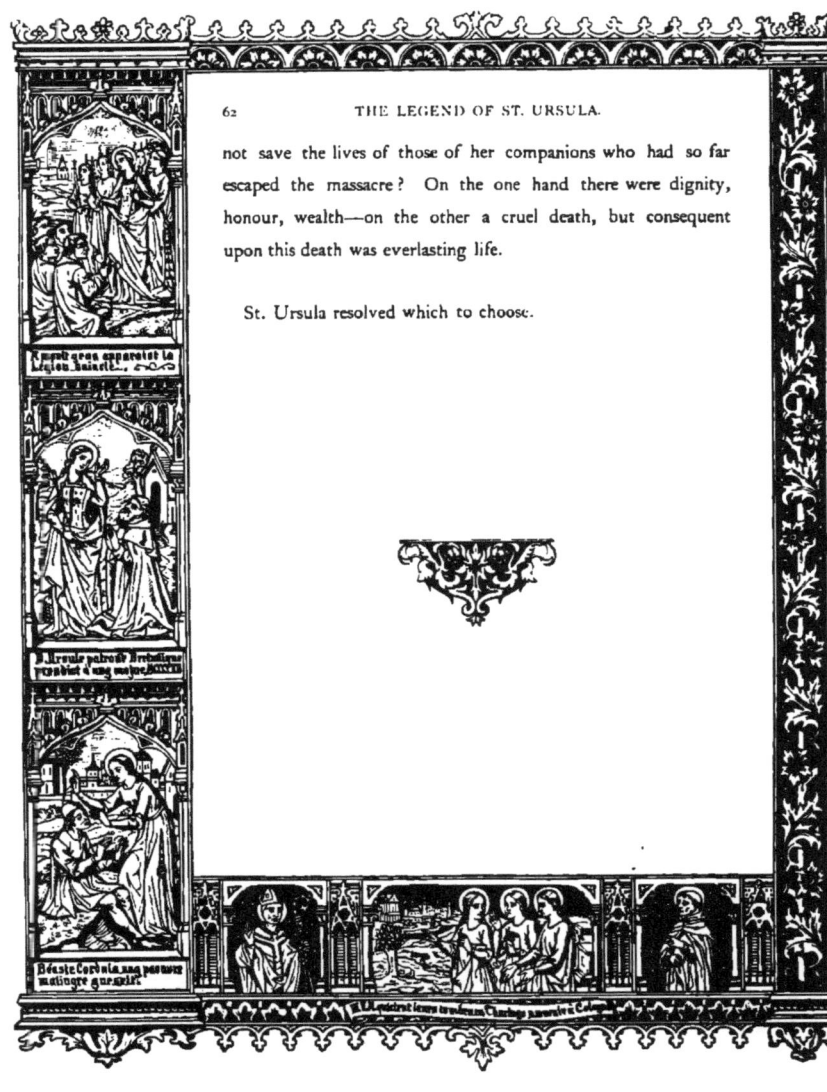

CHAPTER VIII.

ST. URSULA RECEIVES HER CROWN.

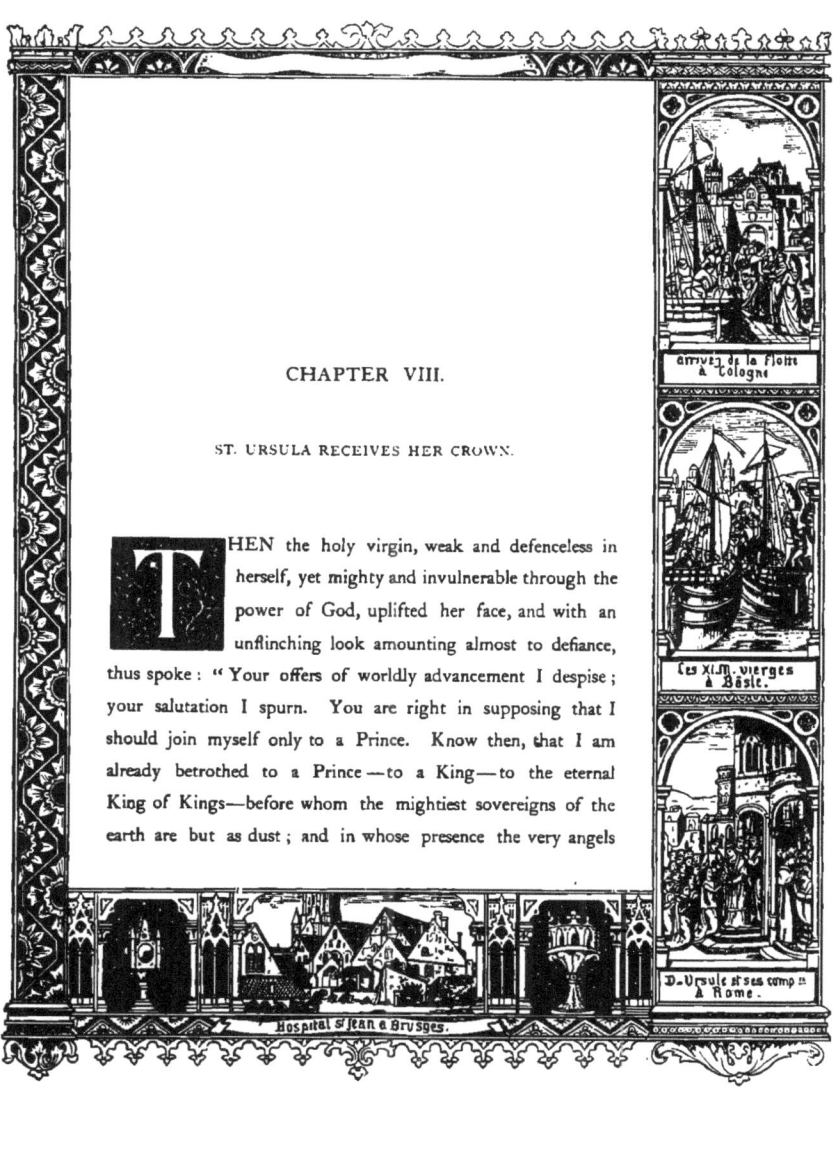

THEN the holy virgin, weak and defenceless in herself, yet mighty and invulnerable through the power of God, uplifted her face, and with an unflinching look amounting almost to defiance, thus spoke: " Your offers of worldly advancement I despise; your salutation I spurn. You are right in supposing that I should join myself only to a Prince. Know then, that I am already betrothed to a Prince — to a King — to the eternal King of Kings — before whom the mightiest sovereigns of the earth are but as dust; and in whose presence the very angels

veil their faces. He it is to whom I have plighted my troth: He is waiting now with outstretched arms to receive me unto Himself, and shall I refuse to obey the summons which calls me to my heavenly nuptials? No! Were I assured that by renouncing my faith the power and wealth of all the kingdoms of the earth would be mine, I would reject them as I do your offer now."

Aasvahs was furious at these words of Ursula. Snatching a spear from the hand of one who stood near, and trembling with rage, he advanced towards the blessed virgin as though he would himself be her executioner; but he, the victorious barbarian, the conqueror of Western Europe, quailed beneath the glance of the spotless maiden who stood before him. By a simple gesture of the hand she motioned him to silence while she proceeded with her answer. The tyrant abashed, was compelled to obey.

"Though I have dedicated my soul to God," Ursula continued with unabated firmness, "my body is in your power. Do with it as you please. Think not that torments would induce me to alter my resolution. Death, the King of Terrors, will be to me as a welcome harbinger of joy. Wreak, then, your

THE LEGEND OF ST. URSULA.

impotent rage on my poor body ; the passage from this life will be but the entrance to another, where happiness and peace shall reign for evermore."

Maddened beyond bounds at the contemptuous rejection of his offer, the tyrant determined to try whether threats would be of more avail. He accordingly ordered those of the blessed band, who in consequence of the darkness had escaped the massacre, to be bound together, and in this helpless position to be given over to the brutality of the soldiers. St. Ursula prayed fervently to heaven while the bloody scene was being enacted, and constantly urged her companions to remain faithful to their vows. Meanwhile the ferocious mob added every refinement to the torture which their ingenuity could suggest ; but death speedily put a period to the sufferings of the defenceless victims, and in a short time of all that noble band none but Ursula was left alive.

"See," said Aasvahs, turning towards her with savage exultation, "such shall be your fate. You are now alone upon the earth, and there remains but one alternative by which you can save yourself. For the last time I ask you which you will

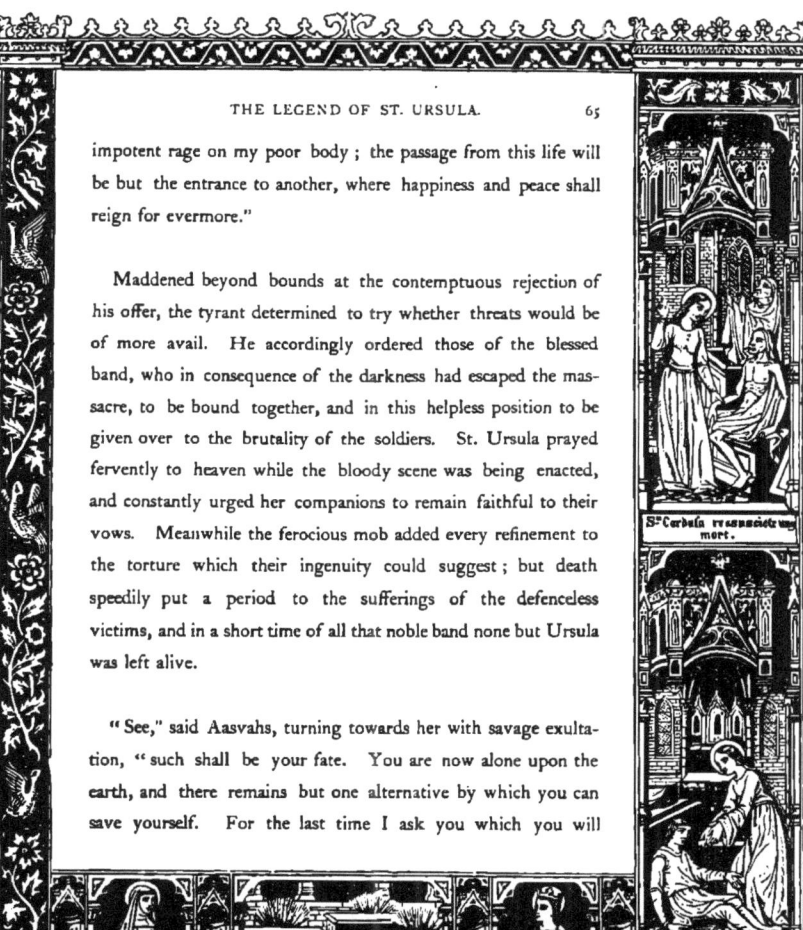

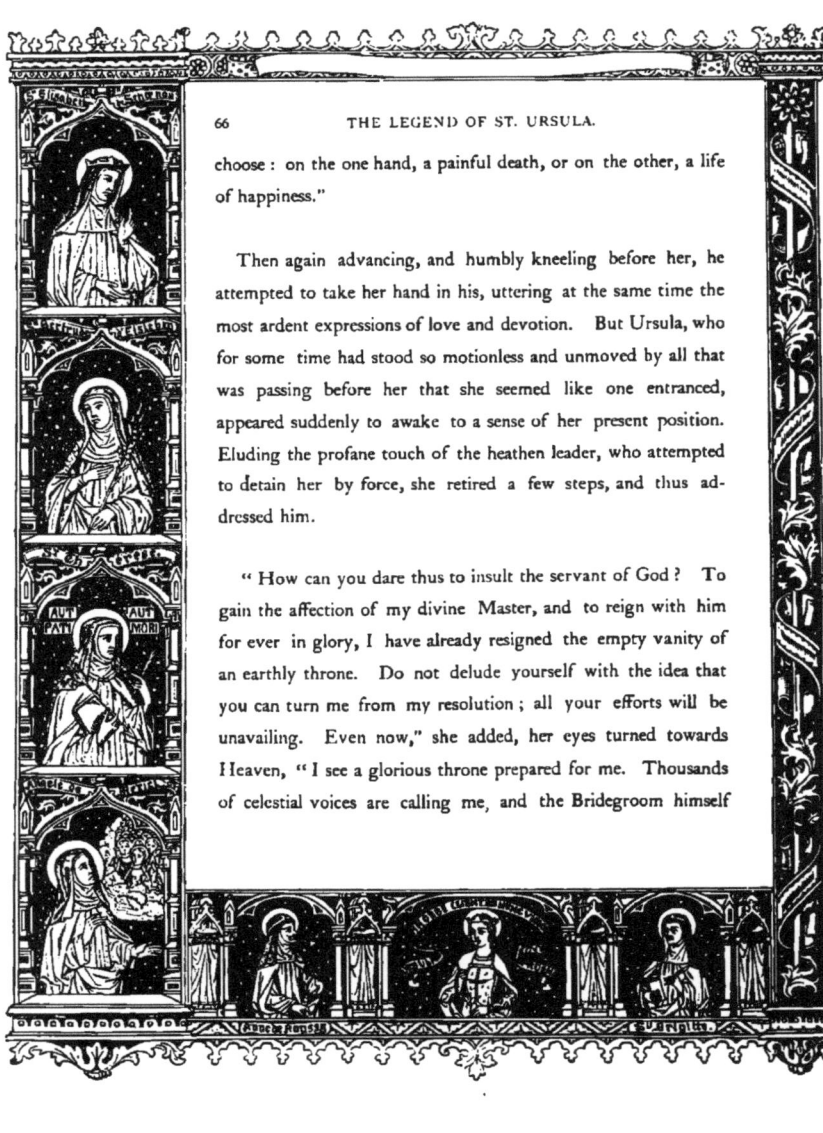

choose: on the one hand, a painful death, or on the other, a life of happiness."

Then again advancing, and humbly kneeling before her, he attempted to take her hand in his, uttering at the same time the most ardent expressions of love and devotion. But Ursula, who for some time had stood so motionless and unmoved by all that was passing before her that she seemed like one entranced, appeared suddenly to awake to a sense of her present position. Eluding the profane touch of the heathen leader, who attempted to detain her by force, she retired a few steps, and thus addressed him.

"How can you dare thus to insult the servant of God? To gain the affection of my divine Master, and to reign with him for ever in glory, I have already resigned the empty vanity of an earthly throne. Do not delude yourself with the idea that you can turn me from my resolution; all your efforts will be unavailing. Even now," she added, her eyes turned towards Heaven, "I see a glorious throne prepared for me. Thousands of celestial voices are calling me, and the Bridegroom himself

THE LEGEND OF ST URSULA. 67

beckons me towards him. Torture me—kill me, if you will—nothing shall induce me to deny my heavenly Master."

At these words the fury of Aasvahs knew no bounds. Springing to his feet, he ordered her, before whom he had just been humbly kneeling, to be immediately put to death. The holy martyr walked to the spot to which she was directed with as much alacrity as if she were summoned to a party of pleasure —nay, more—for the festival to which she was now proceeding was one of which the enjoyment was unalloyed and eternal. At the command of the barbarian leader a soldier shot an arrow at the devoted virgin ; but, being disconcerted at the firmness of her demeanour, he missed his aim, and the bolt only wounded her right arm. Her sacred blood streamed forth, dyeing with its crimson stain her robe and the spotless ermine which enriched it. Even in this trying moment, while her strength was rapidly failing, and her life oozing from the wound, her fortitude did not for one instant desert her. Instead of repining, she thanked her Almighty Father that she was deemed worthy to suffer for His sake, and was heard to exclaim that her pain was as nothing to that which her blessed Saviour endured to redeem her soul from hell.

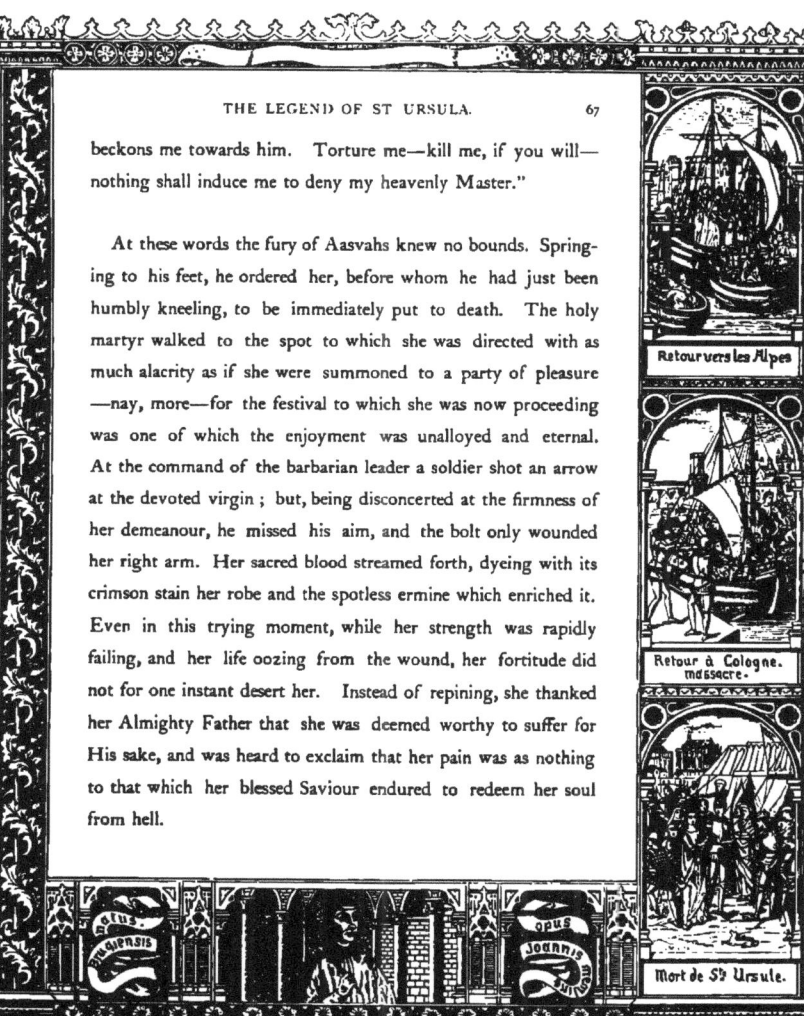

THE LEGEND OF ST. URSULA.

A second arrow was fitted to the string, and swift as lightning sped on its fatal mission. St. Ursula was standing with outstretched arms, her face directed heavenwards, as if eager to enjoy its rest, when the arrow pierced her heart, and her happy soul, released from its earthly tenement, winged its glorious flight to be for ever with Him whom she delighted to serve on earth. A deadly fear fell upon all around; for the sweet strains of music were heard; a delicious perfume seemed to exhale from the earth; and a cloud of dazzling brightness shone upon the spot where lay the corpses of the virgin martyrs —the Bridegroom was welcoming his affianced bride.

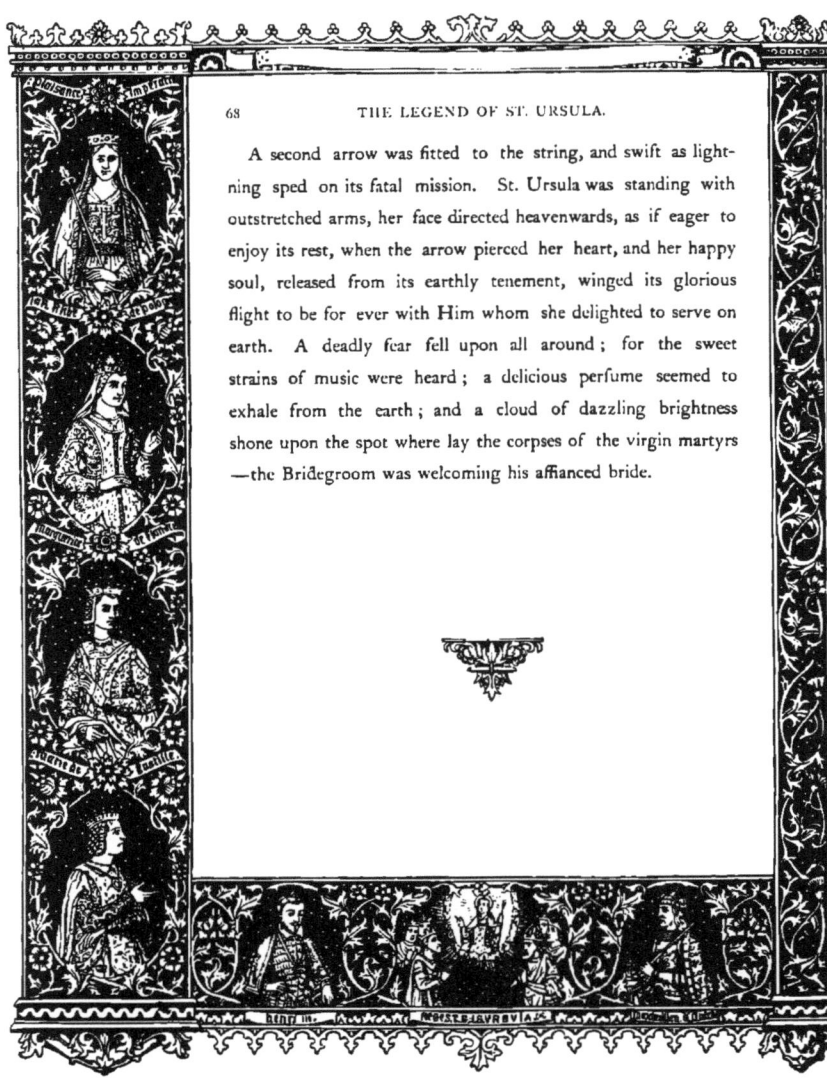

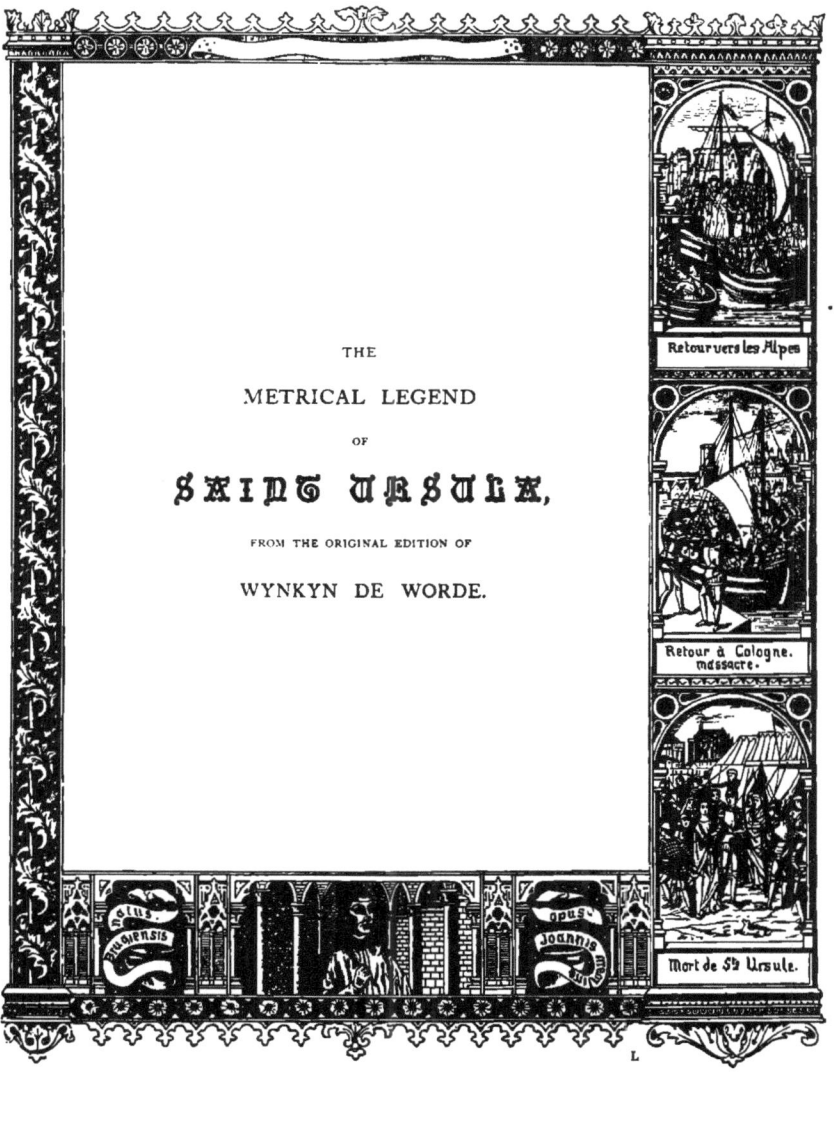

THE METRICAL LEGEND
OF
SAINT URSULA,
FROM THE ORIGINAL EDITION OF
WYNKYN DE WORDE.

The following Metrical Version of the Legend of St. Ursula was written towards the close of the Fifteenth Century, by Edmund Hatfield, a Monk of Rochester. It was dedicated to the most Illustrious Lady Margaret, the Mother of King Henry the Seventh, and was one of the earliest works which issued from the press of Wynkyn de Worde.

In 1818, the Roxburghe Club produced an exquisite facsimile of this most curious book, from an original copy in the possession of the Duke of Devonshire. The reprint is now extremely *rare*, only thirty-two copies having been printed—of which one was on vellum—for distribution amongst the members of the Club.

Dévostes Ursulines
resconfortées par
Notre Dame.

With constant cure eschewynge Ignoraunce
 With stedfast studye frome errour to applye
 With modest mynde to withstande varyaūce
Cryste with thy comforte Illumyn me lucydently
Of Ursula virgyn the lyfe to veryfye
In laudynge her and for our informacyon
With grace I purpose playnly to pateſye
The lyfe and londe where she had her creacyon

In the yere of god thre hondred thyrty and twayne
By ye romayns conquest brytayne was in subgeccyon
Thrughe a noble cayptayne named Marimian
Whiche kepte this londe longe vnder his correccyon
By force dysinheret the blode of trewe eleccyon
Put Conan meriedok from all his dygnyte
Whiche sholde haue ruled this lode vnd· his pteccyon
Of the blode royall dyscendynge lynyally

Than to recompence this Conan meriedocke
Marimian conquered the londe of amorican
And gaue it to Conan his tytell to reuoke
Whiche for the conquest was named lytell brytayne
Syth of the romayns the hole empyre he wan
Takynge from brytayne the chefe men of estate
To strength his warres he lefte no valyaunt man
So were the nobles from brytayne segregate

He lefte Dyonothus grete brytayne to protecte
Fader unto Ursula and kynge of cornewall
This Conan meriedok to cornewall dyde dyrecte
For wyues of brytayne and Ursula in especyall
Whiche sente by shyppe a company birgynall
Ri. thousande maydens & thre score thousande wyues
Within the tymes they toke theyr passage all
Whiche by grete tepest ye moost parte lose theyr lyues

Saue all the birgyns arryued within the rynde
Amonge the hoost of Gwanus and duke melgye
Bycause they wolde not fulfyll the tyrauntes mynde
There they were quelled by the henaudes furyously
Thrugh this occasyon Gwanus wente to the see
And londed in brytayne bsurpynge the prynceppate
Wastynge the chyrche with force and cruelte
So sayth the cronycles for our certyfycate

Her hystory or legende these cronycles doth impunge
In the yere of god two hondred thyrty and eyght
Sayenge that .ri.M. birgyns bothe olde and yonge
Were quelled at colen by henaudes without fyght
With Cyryake pope and dyuers men of myght
But in my mynde this was chefe cause of baryaunce
Whan Gwanus in brytayne deposed ordre & ryght
So he dystroyed all bokes of allegaunce

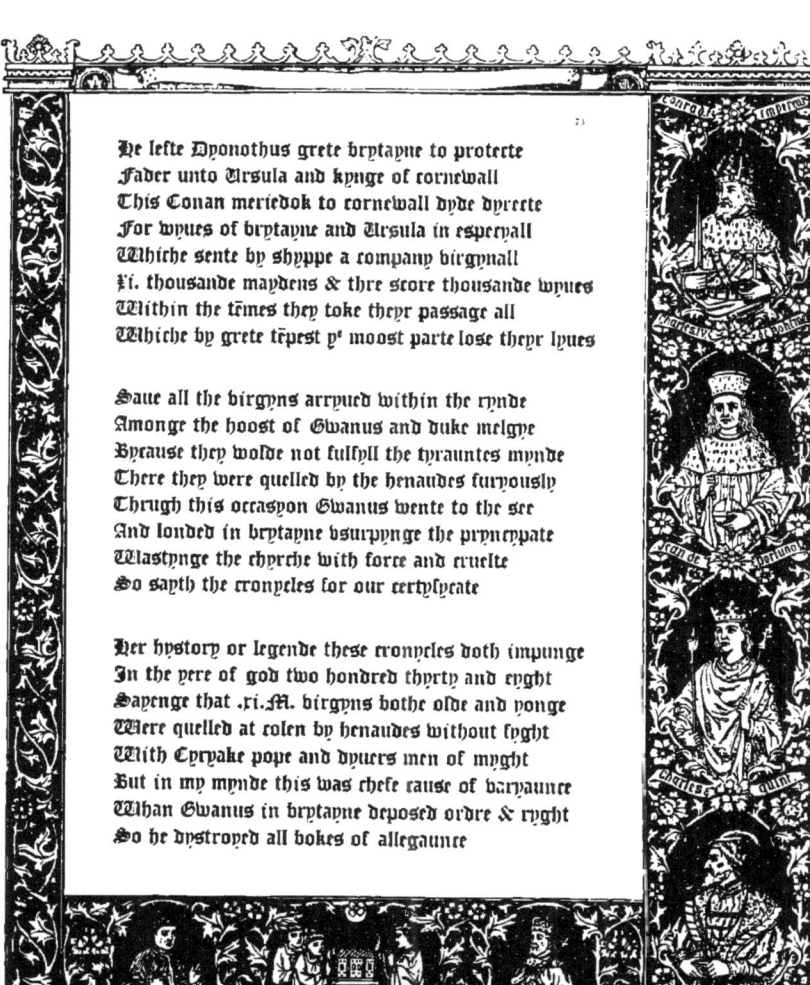

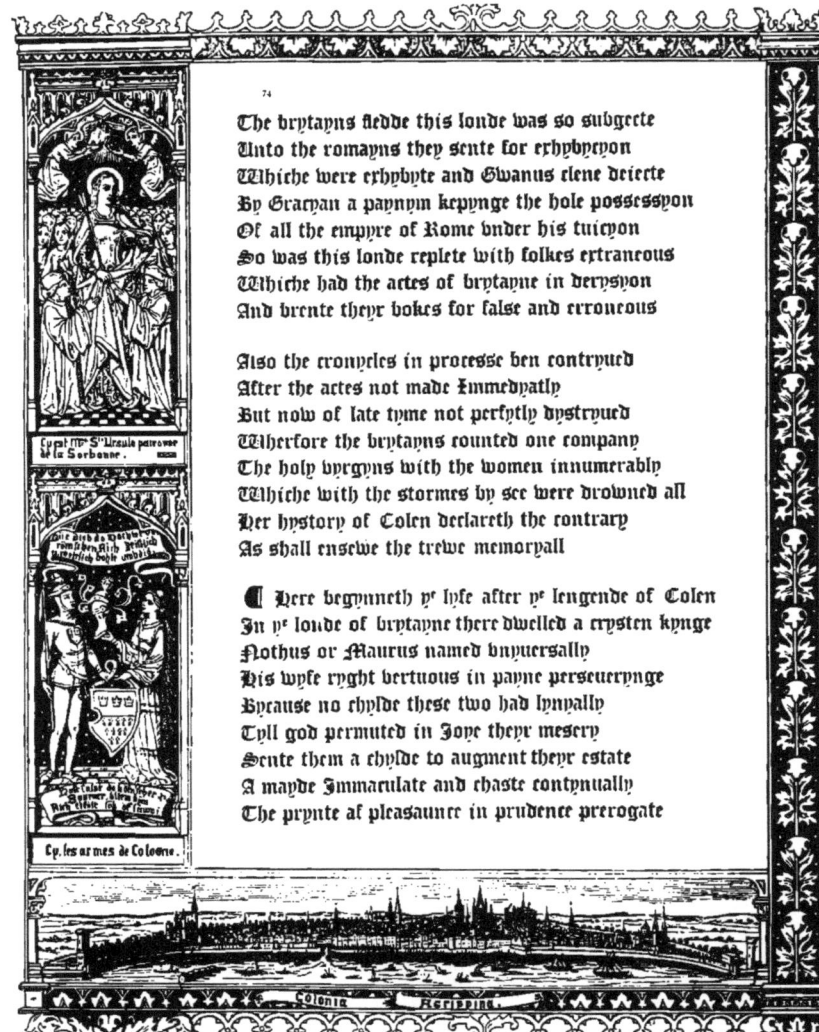

The brytayns fledde this londe was so subgecte
Unto the romayns they sente for exhybycyon
Whiche were exhybyte and Gwanus clene deiecte
By Gracyan a paynym kepynge the hole possessyon
Of all the empyre of Rome vnder his tuicyon
So was this londe replete with folkes extraneous
Whiche had the actes of brytayne in derysyon
And brente theyr bokes for false and erroneous

Also the cronycles in processe ben contryued
After the actes not made Immedyatly
But now of late tyme not perfytly dystryued
Wherfore the brytayns counted one company
The holy vyrgyns with the women innumerably
Whiche with the stormes by see were drowned all
Her hystory of Colen declareth the contrary
As shall ensewe the trewe memoryall

℘ Here begynneth yᵉ lyfe after yᵉ lengende of Colen
In yᵉ londe of brytayne there dwelled a crysten kynge
Nothus or Maurus named vnyuersally
His wyfe ryght vertuous in payne perseueryuge
Bycause no chylde these two had lynyally
Tyll god permuted in Joye theyr mesery
Sente them a chylde to augment theyr estate
A mayde Immaculate and chaste contynually
The prynte of pleasaunce in prudence prerogate

This vyrgyn in vertue venerable
Was named Ursula heyre apparent to the lande
Of courage constaunte in cryst incomparable
Of her vyrgynyte to hym she made a bande
To brynge her lampe Illumynate in her hande
Protecte electe abierte frone bylanye
That of her persone all pryncs dyde demaunde
Them to assocyate to her vyrgynytye

The fructuous fame the fayrnes of flos mundi
Was spredde ouer all how she was preelecte
Quia civitas supra montem nequit absconditi
So that a tyraunt a paynym dyde her affecte
The kynge of brytayne moost souerayne of that secte
Unto his sone of her despderatyue
Sente supplycaryons with thretenynge to deiecte
Nothus her fader yf he were negatyue

This noble Nothus sore meued in his mynde
To this demaunde no responce coude deuyse
Bycause his doughter to cryst her corps dyde bynde
And to the paynym he durst make no prompse
He fered his fury his londe wolde enterpryse
Thus gyue his aunswere he stode without counsell
Tyll that his doughter vertuous of words and wyse
Out of his herte all anger dyde expell

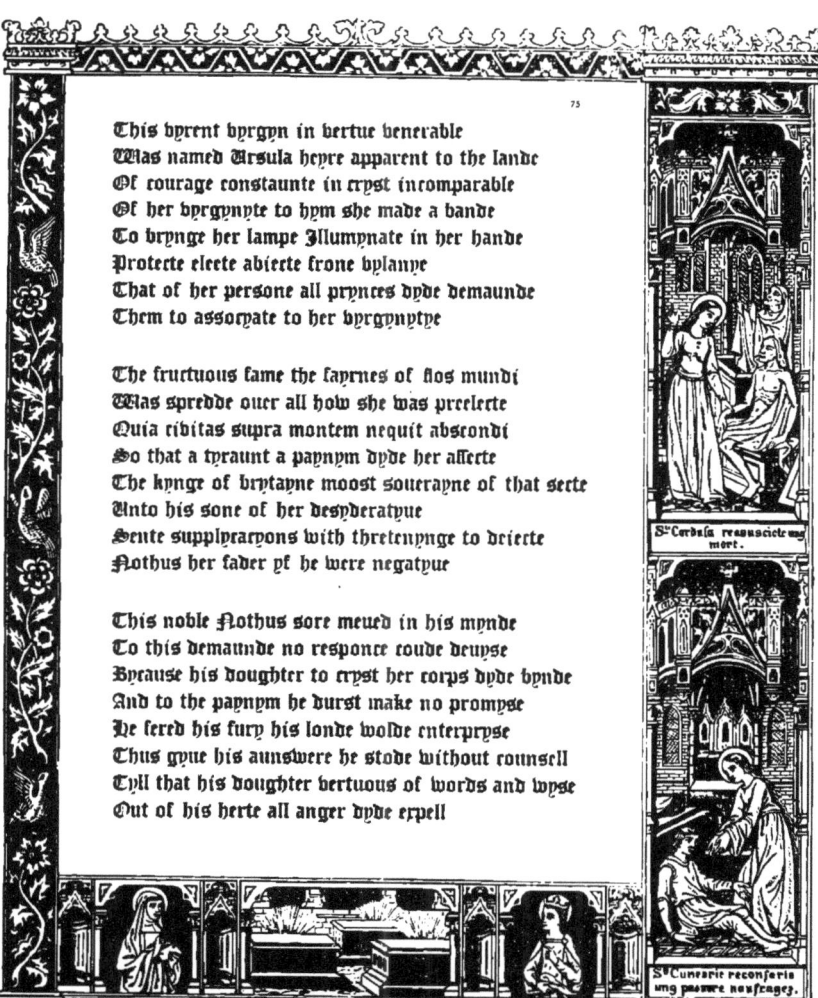

St Cordula reassuscicie ung
mort.

St Cunerie reconforie
ung pauure naufrage.

With prudence prompte to make contracte content
As she was taught by dyuyne ammonycyon
Afore her fader she sayd she wolde consent
To wedde this prynce reseruynge this condycyon
That he were crystened grauntange an other petycyon
Of thre yeres space that he myght be instructe
Sendynge of birgyns .r. under my tuicyon
To every birgyn a thousande moo conducte

The letter myssyues sealed by noble Nothus
Immedyately in Englonde they were dyrecte
The sense therof pleased the prynce Ethereus
And prayed his fader to perfourme the effecte
That for that lady his ydolles he wolde deiecte
To this peycyon his fader dyde applye
And sought ouer all for birgyns preelecte
Of bothe the landes his mynde to satysfye

In lyke wyse Nothus puruayed on his partye
For shyppes & stuffe to perfourme theyr hole passage
And maryners good to kepe them company
With certayne women to gyue them better courage
And thus the birgyns gadred of euery age
Of euery partye resorte grete confluence
Some poore some ryche and some of hye lygnage
Her hystory and legende sheweth suche euydence

Than Nothus sendynge a message vnto Gerasen
The quene of cicile shewed her of all the facyon
Saynt Ursulaes aunt and syster to the quene
Whiche cristened her husbāde by her swete exortaciōn
Chaungynge his tyranny in crystes contemplacyon
She came to brytayne with her sone Adryan
And her foure doughters of heuenly conuersacyon
Victoryn Babilla Aure and Julyan

The reuerent rumor thrugh out all realmes reygned
With kynges and quenes and lordes of estate
With dyuers bisshoppes \bout theyr nōbre assygned
By confluence grete with them were assocyate
Grete Joye it was to them congregate
That all the worlde of theyr fame was replenysshed
Hunger nor colde theyr bodyes dyde abate
Unto the tyme that thre yere were full fynysshed

To accompte theyr lygnage it were longe to procede
But of the pryncypall I purpose to dyscryue
Ryght as the hystory and legende doth me lede
To study theron it were contemplatyue
For of the birgyns I entende to contryue
With nōbre of kynges & bysshoppes of grete honour
To folowe these birgyns theyr dygnyte dyd depryue
It was grete solace to se these sayntes in ordour

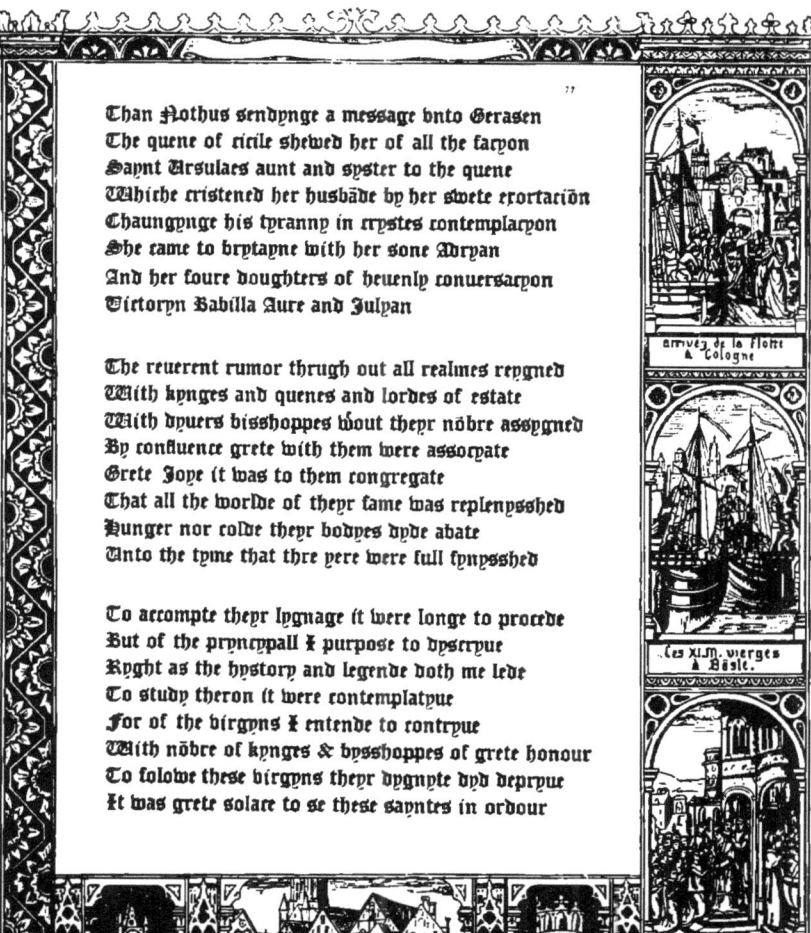

arrivez de la flotte à Cologne

Les XI.M. vierges à Basle.

D. Ursule et ses comp^s à Rome.

Hospital St Jean a Bruges.

Nothus reioysed to se the congregacyon
Augmentynge dayly in cryste our fayth catholyke
Theyr bertuous lyuynge theyr loue theyr couersaciō
Theyr heuenly lust replete with fode aungelyke
That of theyr praysynge the psalmist dyde pronostike
Quia perfecisti laudem ex ore infancium
Confourmynge well the wordes euangelyke
Quod birgines prudentes portabant oleum

Theyr holy names to expresse I entende
Of all the prynceppall after the trewe hystory
Tho that I can not in ryme all comprehende
Labour the entent and lette the sounde passe by
Theyr holy names to the ryme may not applye
To bary the sense for soundynge of a syllable
I holde not best leste some wolde thynke contrary
And Iuge this wrytynge forged or fallyble

℄ The names of virgyns.
Aboue all other these fyue were prynceppall
Ursula was fyrst to cryste that cast her courage
The nexte Aynnosa of her orygynall
Cordula the thyrde doughter of an erle sage
Her legende sheweth she was of Ursulaes lygnage
The fourth Elutheria doughter to Ursulaes aunt
The fyfth Florencia ryght wyse but yonge of age
Doughter of a kynge in y^e fayth of cryste flagraunt

tombeau de St Ursule á Cologne.

After these fyue .xi. more were electe
To be chefe guydes the other to conducte
With dyuers matrones the chyldren to pretecte
Bothe preestes and clerkes the women to instructe
Some were small babes that of theyr moders sucte
Aungelles for comforte with them were conuersaunt
And deuylles also these virgyns seducte
Promysed grete ryches but they abode constaunt

The fyrst was Iothathe doughter of a kynge
With her two systers Gempnyan and Iustyce
Whiche had a thousande byrgyns in her guydynge
The seconde Benygna whiche had a semblable offyce
With Sybyll Mobyll Eufrosyn and Custyce
All foure her systers of a duke procreate
The thyrde Clemencia doughter to an erle of pryce
Julian and Inducta her systers assocyate

The fourth Sapiencia doughter of a prynce prudent
With her two systers Eulalia and Serene
The fyfth Carpasora of a kynge procedent
With Eutropped & Pallidore systers & byrgyns clene
The syxte Columba to a thousande dyde preuene
With Cordula her syster of a kynge generate
The seuenth Benedicta with her foure systers shene
To her obedyence a thousand congregate

The eyght Odilia of a grete erle dyscended
With systers twayne Ursicia and Juliana
To her proteccyon a thousande were commaunded
The nynth Celindris with her syster Virgilia
Borne of a kynge, the tenth was Sibilia
With her thre systers a thousande had to cure
Named Juliana Luria and Eugenia
All kynges doughters and birgyns clene and pure

The .xi. Lucia of corps and bertue benuste
Ryght nye of kynne to the prynce Ethereus
Under her guydynge she had a thousande Juste
With Placida her syster a birgyn beauteous
These .xi. birgyns in cryste so courageous
Aboue all other possessed the pryncypate
They spente theyr tyme in sportes ryght bertuous
No game was lefte amonge them improbate

❡ The names of bysshoppes.

The nombre of bysshoppes I purpose to patefye
That with these birgyns suffred theyr martyrdome
Fyue out of Englonde came to this company
Fyrst was Willms of holy conuersacyon
Jacobus his brother went with the congregacyon
And bysshoppes bothe and vncles to Ursula
The thyrde Ywanus borne of the same nacyon
Well aged and vncle to birgyn Eulalia

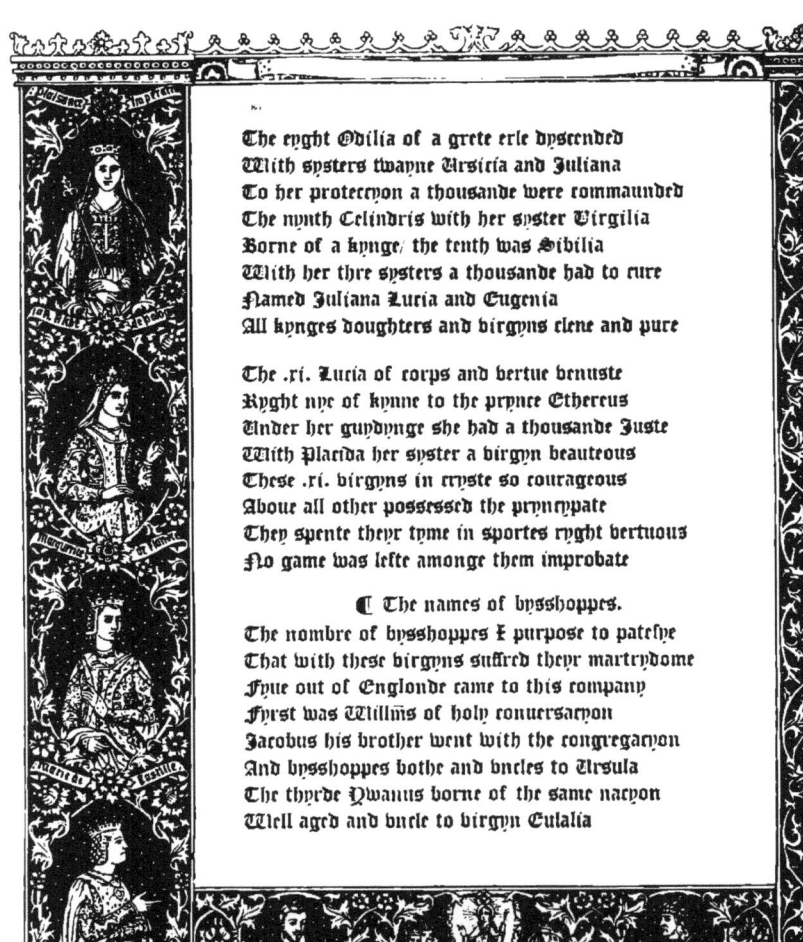

The fourth Eleutherius / the fyfth Lotharius hyght
To the prynce Etherius ryght nye of lygnage
Also the bysshoppe of methe with all his myght
Named Mauricius mette them in theyr byage
He hasted hym to wynne the heuenly gage
To Ursulales moder brother her was germayne
With Panthalus bysshop and guyde in theyr passage
Brought them to Rome & syth frome Rome agayne.

Of .riii. kynges her hystorye doth expresse
Of whiche I purpose theyr names to notefye
Besechynge hertely the reders to redresse
Theyr eeres to god and to flee ypocrysye
Some man wolde thynke that thystorye doth lye
That so many kynges sholde dye withouten fyght
Remembre of olde that cronycles berefye
That many a lorde was called a kynge of myght

℄ The names of kynges.
Bycause of dygnyte a kynges sone named a kynge
A dukes sone a duke and so forth conformable
Not than as now one in a londe reygnynge
Wherof Ethereus in fayth bothe ferme and stable
Prynce of grete brytayne of Ursula spousable
Not in theyr passage to Rome assocyate
But as the aungell admytte hym acceptable
To be with his spouse in passyon copulate

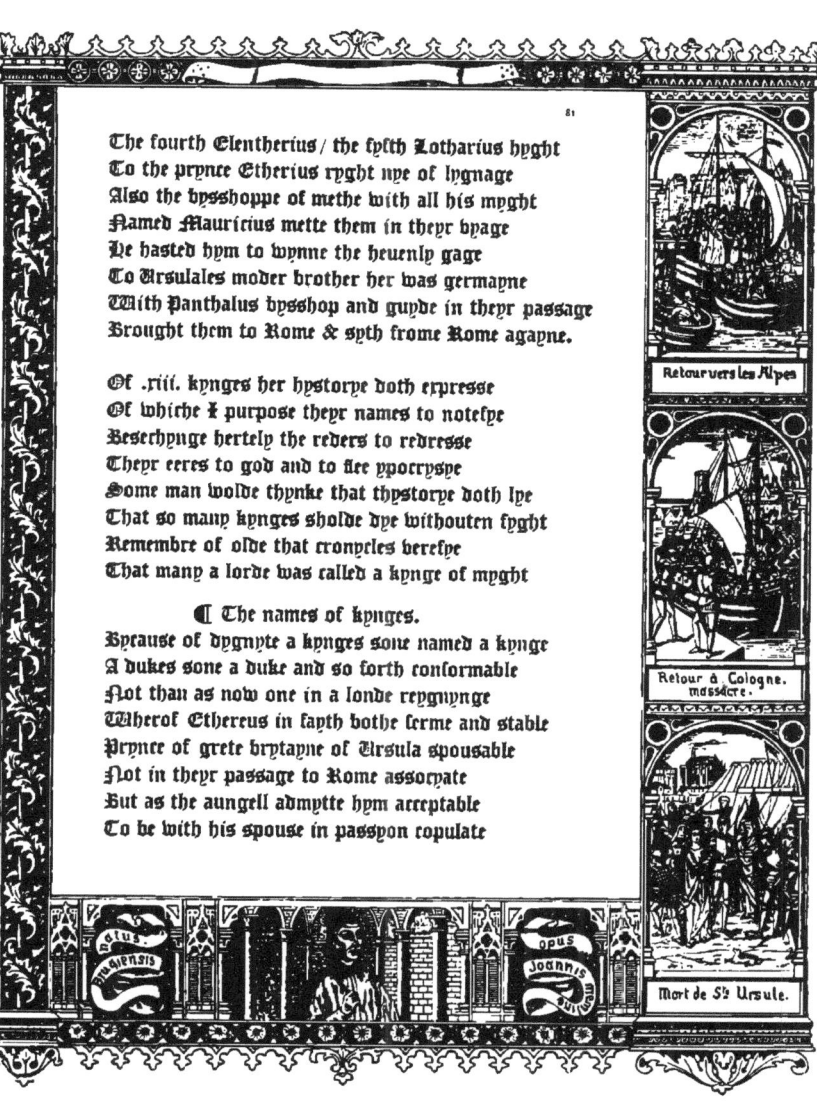

Retour vers les Alpes

Retour à Cologne. massacre.

Mort de Ste Ursule.

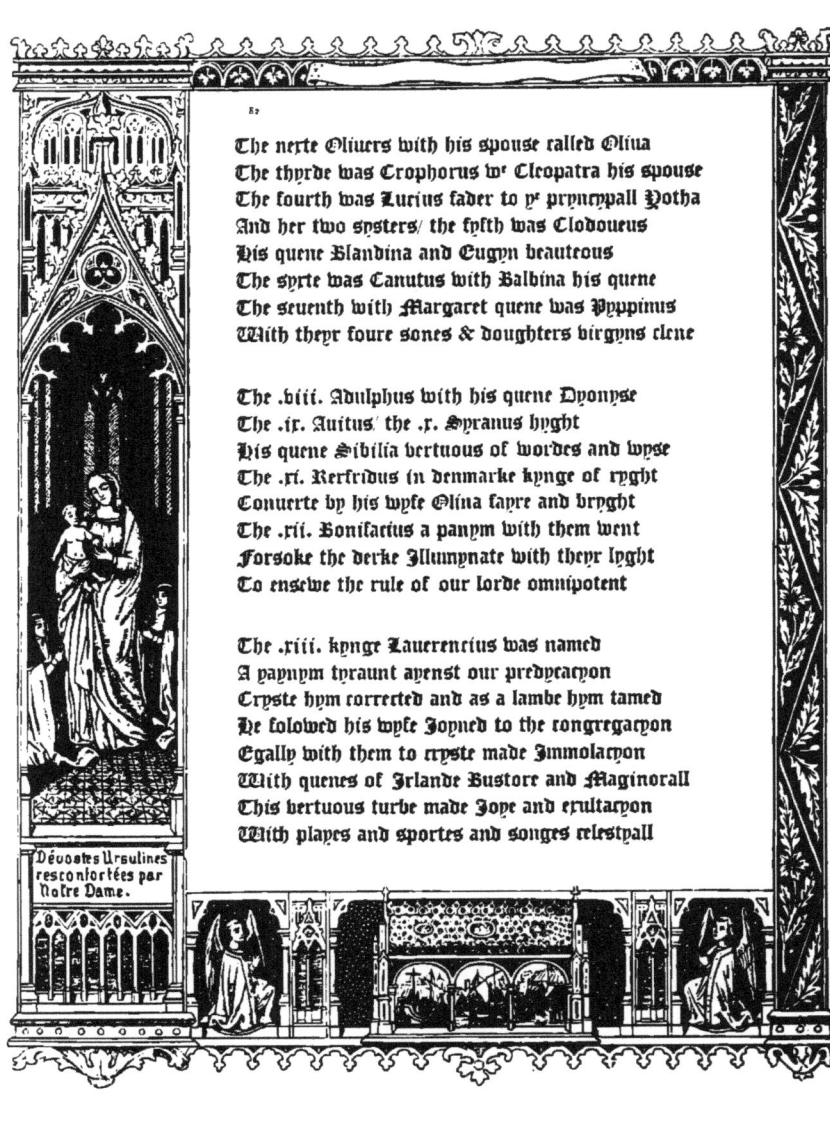

The nexte Oliuers with his spouse called Oliua
The thyrde was Crophorus wt Cleopatra his spouse
The fourth was Lucius fader to ye pryncypall Yotha
And her two systers/ the fyfth was Clodoueus
His quene Blandina and Eugyn beauteous
The syxte was Canutus with Balbina his quene
The seuenth with Margaret quene was Pyppinus
With theyr foure sones & doughters birgyns clene

The .viii. Adulphus with his quene Dyonyse
The .ix. Auitus, the .x. Spranus hyght
His quene Sibilia bertuous of wordes and wyse
The .xi. Rerfridus in denmarke kynge of ryght
Conuerte by his wyfe Olina fayre and bryght
The .xii. Bonifacius a panym with them went
Forsoke the derke Illumynate with theyr lyght
To ensewe the rule of our lorde omnipotent

The .xiii. kynge Lauerencius was named
A paynym tyraunt ayenst our predycacyon
Cryste hym corrected and as a lambe hym tamed
He folowed his wyfe Joyned to the congregacyon
Egally with them to cryste made Immolacyon
With quenes of Irlande Bustore and Maginorall
This bertuous turbe made Joye and exultacyon
With playes and sportes and songes celestyall

Dévostes Ursulines
resconfortées par
Notre Dame.

Some man wolde aske how all these were susteyned
Where myght ye bytaylles be founde for so lōge space
He that to moyses manna in the deserte reyned
Myght them all satisfye with his perpetuall grace
They were appayred neyther in body nor in face
In clothynge labour in sykenes yonge nor olde
In all theyr Journay welcomed in euery place
The gyftes of god be moderate many folde

Thus in theyr shyppes these sayntes celestyall
Sayled for solace and londed euery nyght
Tyll that our lorde to his courte dyde them call
With boryall blastes dyde stratche theyr sayles tyght
To be theyr guydes he sente his aungelles bryght
Athwarte the see by his dyuyne prouysyon
Brought them to haue thrugh his immoderat myght
In the porte of tilia preserued in his tuicyon

This porte is sette besyde the mouth of the rynde
Where they were charged by the celestyall message
To sayle to Colen with the occydentall wynde
Theyr shyppes were prest to perfourme theyr passage
Ayenst the streme to Colen chose theyr byage
That .viii. dayes saylynge the thyrde day dyd cōplete
Therwith the archebysshopp & all the cyteyzyns sage
Reuerently they were receyued in euery strete

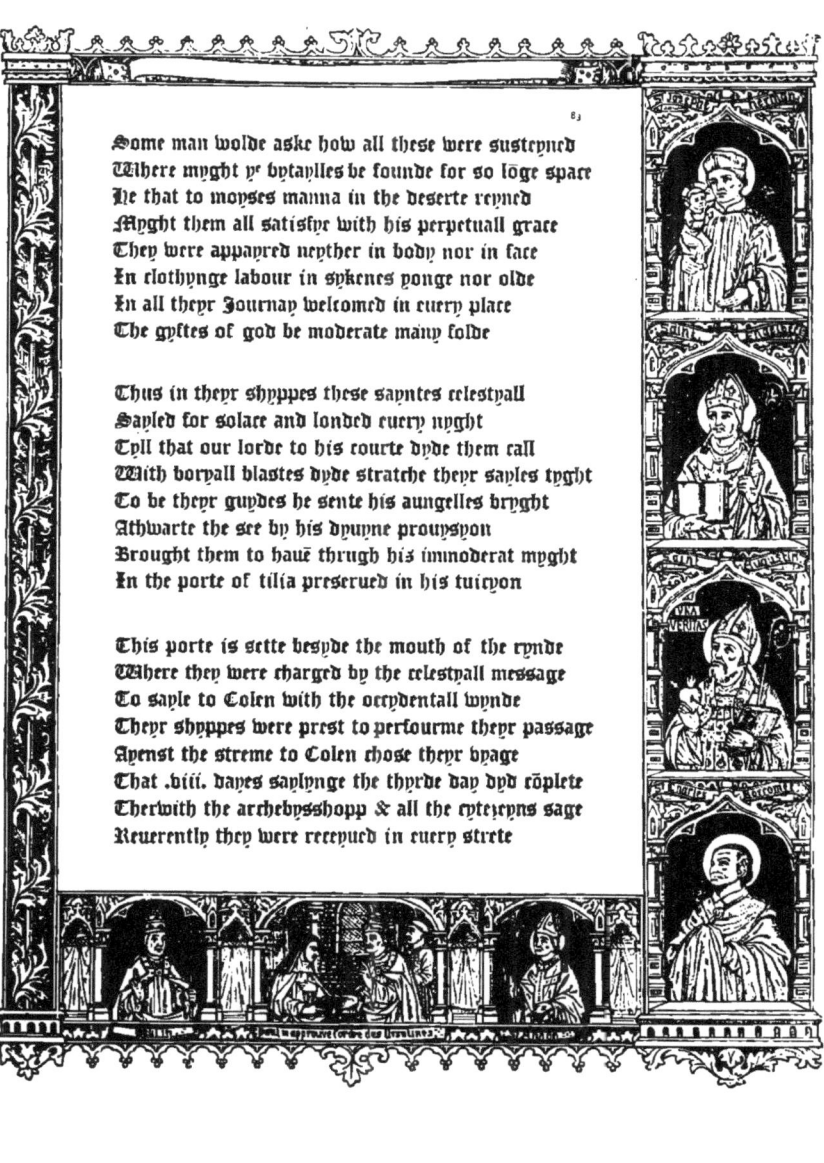

And there a whyle these birgyns them reposed
Tyll that an aungell comaunded them to remeue
And bysyte Rome wherof the turbe reioysed
Thākynge yͤ archebysshopp, & cytezens toke theyrleue
They dressed theyr shyppes their passage for to preue
And sayled thre dayes swyftely ayenst the rynde
Or none the fourth daye at basyle dyde arryue
Well .viii. dayes saylynge by force of behemēt wynde

At theyr dyscendynge receyued reuerently
Of Panthalus bysshop and all the cytezeyns
Gretely reioysed to se suche a company
Strengthynge our fayth by so grete confluence
Takynge theyr Iournay with herte & dylygence
To rome on fote that were so tender of age
This Panthalus thought his synne to recompence
Hym to assocyate with them in theyr byage

These holy birgyns to rome made theyr progressyon
And Panthalus bysshop with his affynytye
The maydens wente by couples in processyon
In vertuous talkynge theyr mynde dyde satysfye
They suffred no payne passynge the mountayns hye
No horse nor carte to them were erigent
Saue kynges and bysshoppes had in theyr company
An hondred horse to cary theyr arayment

No rayne nor tempest made them impedyment
Frome theyr departynge out of the palays of nothus
Unto the tyme that cryste omnipotent
Dyde them inupte vnto his realme so gloryous
Thus in shorte space they came all Joyous
Within a daye of Rome all congregate
They mette with the reuerent fader in god Cesarius
The bysshoppe of myllan to them assocyate

  ¶ Here they came to Rome
To rome they came theyr reuerence for to make
Where they were receyued ryght solemply w pression
With all his cardynalles there came the pope ciriake
Unto saynt Peters they made theyr fyrst processyon
The pope was gladde to se theyr conuersacyon
For he of Brytayne had his orygynall
And bincent cardynall borne of the same nacyon
Many of theyr lygnage amonge the birgyns small

Some of the maydens that were not baptysed
The pope complete in them the sacrament
Euery day prechynge holyly aduertysed
Tyll that our lorde an aungell to hym sente
And tolde the pope that it was expedyente
That he sholde resygne to Antherus his renowme
And folowe these byrgyns to Colen in this entente
There to receyue the crowne of martyrdome

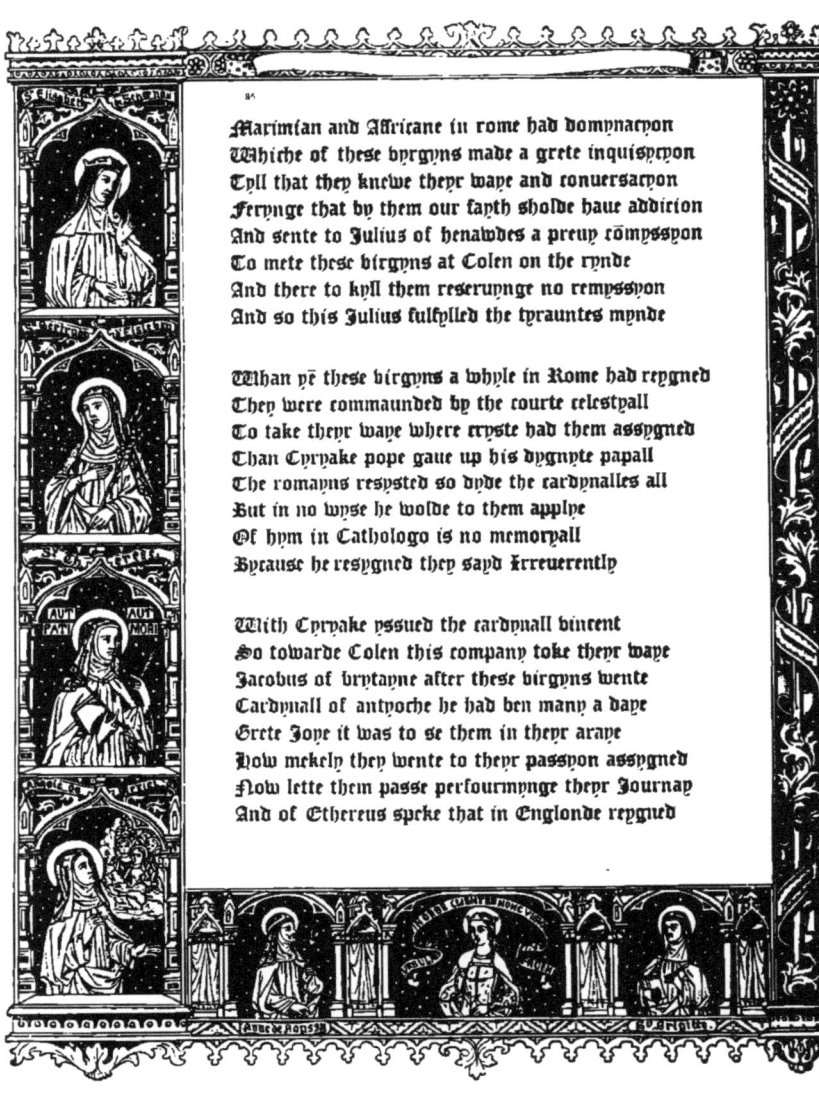

Marimian and Affricane in rome had dompnacyon
Whiche of these byrgyns made a grete inquisycyon
Tyll that they knewe theyr waye and conuersacyon
Ferynge that by them our fayth sholde haue addicion
And sente to Julius of henawdes a preuy cōmpssyon
To mete these birgyns at Colen on the rynde
And there to kyll them reserupnge no rempssyon
And so this Julius fulfylled the tyrauntes mynde

Whan yᵉ these birgyns a whyle in Rome had regned
They were commaunded by the courte celestyall
To take theyr waye where crystе had them assygned
Than Cyryake pope gaue up his dygnyte papall
The romayns resysted so dyde the cardynalles all
But in no wyse he wolde to them applye
Of hym in Cathologo is no memoryall
Bycause he resygned they sayd irreuerently

With Cyryake yssued the cardynall bincent
So towarde Colen this company toke theyr waye
Jacobus of brytayne after these birgyns wente
Cardynall of antyoche he had ben many a daye
Grete Joye it was to se them in theyr araye
How mekely they wente to theyr passyon assygned
Now lette them passe perfourmynge theyr Journay
And of Ethereus speke that in Englonde regned

Unto Ethereus an aungell was dyrecte
Commaundynge hym to leue his patrymony
To mete his spouse with her to be electe
Whiche hasted hym to folowe effectuously
He baptysed his moder and his syster solemplye
To mete with Ursula by shyppe they toke passage
Ayenst the rynde to mense the ryche cyte
Therwith the birgyns they mette on theyr byage

Than was Ethereus baptysed by the pope
Whiche afore that tyme by dyuyne ammonycyon
Commaunded was to haue good fayth and hope
And not be crystened but by the popes prouysyon
Than with grete Joye to colen they made regressyon
With Clement ye bysshop with kynges & many a duke
And Merculus bysshop of grece in theyr tuicyon
With them assocyate Follarius bysshop of Luke

This holy turbe to Colen made theyr retourne
All clene confessed prest in theyr pylgrymage
Aboute the cyte the henaudes dyde soiourne
Whiche of the nauy aspyed the hole arryuage
Than Ursula prayed to cryste with all courage
To saue her systers from Sathanys seducyon
Than sente our sauyour a celestyall messuge
Saynt Johny^e euagelyst y^e kepte thē from corrupcyon

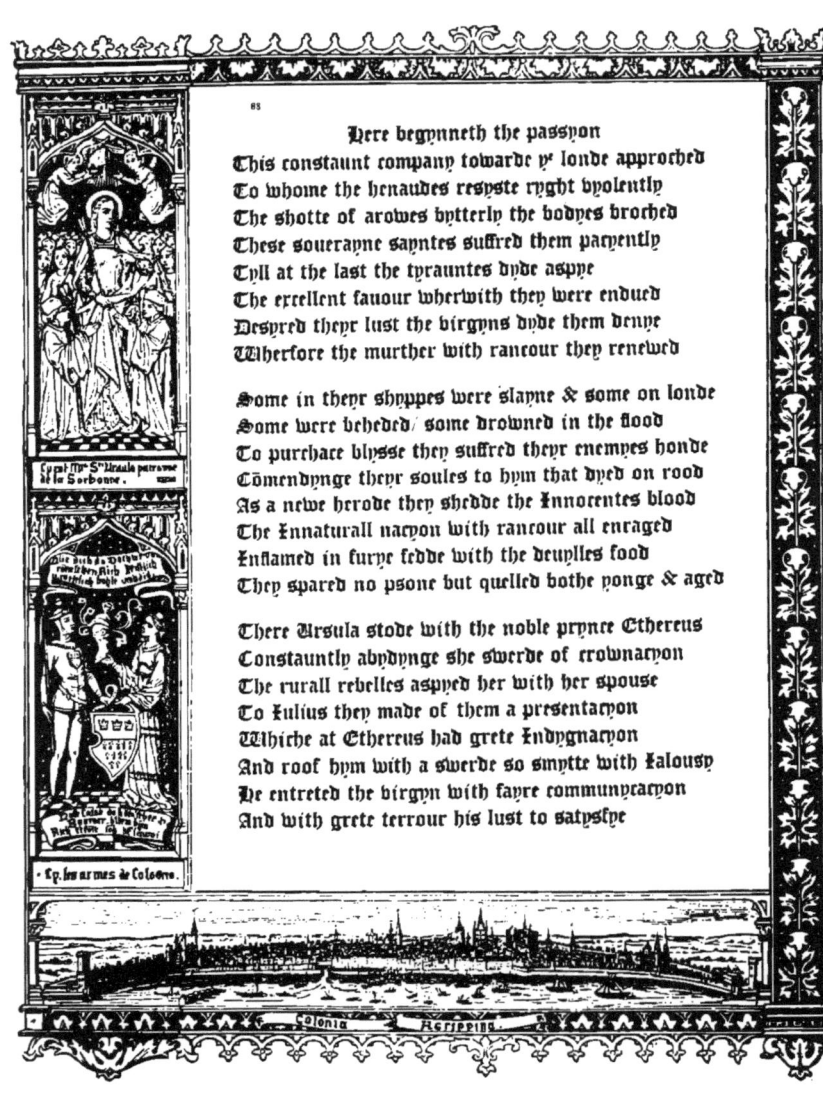

Here begynneth the passyon

This constaunt company towarde yͤ londe approched
To whome the henaudes resyste ryght vyolently
The shotte of arowes bytterly the bodyes broched
These souerayne sayntes suffred them pacyently
Tyll at the last the tyrauntes dyde aspye
The excellent fauour wherwith they were endued
Despyed theyr lust the virgyns dyde them denye
Wherfore the murther with rancour they renewed

Some in theyr shyppes were slayne & some on londe
Some were beheded, some drowned in the flood
To purchace blysse they suffred theyr enemyes honde
Cōmendynge theyr soules to hym that dyed on rood
As a newe herode they shedde the Innocentes blood
The Innaturall nacyon with rancour all enraged
Inflamed in furye fedde with the deuylles food
They spared no psone but quelled bothe yonge & aged

There Ursula stode with the noble prynce Ethereus
Constauntly abydynge she swerde of crownacyon
The rurall rebelles aspyed her with her spouse
To Iulius they made of them a presentacyon
Whiche at Ethereus had grete Indygnacyon
And roof hym with a swerde so smytte with Ialousy
He entreted the virgyn with fayre communycacyon
And with grete terrour his lust to satysfye

This bertuous birgyn abhorred his flesshely proffre
In hym rebukynge with wordes mylde and sage
The seed of sathan her sapyence myght not suffre
But grenned for woo with rancour he began to rage
He drewe an arowe his anger to asswage
And perced the prudent prymerose thrughe ye brayne
Commendynge her soule to cryste with all courage
Thus were these sayntes dysperpled spoyled & slayne

Alas what rumour thrughe out the cyte reygned
To se these birgyns lyenge alonge the streme
So noble lygnage theyr hedes so lowe enclyned
What deth were worthy these cowardes to redempne
Whiche spoyled theyr bodyes of golde & precyous gēme
Aboute the cyte as the psalmyst declareth
Effuderunt bt aquam sanctorum sanguinem
In circuitu Ierusalem et non est qui sepeliret

All were deiecte excepte one Cordula
Whiche ferynge deth dyde her in a shyppe ly lowe
She kepte her secrete tyll on the seconde daye
Than she behelde her systers lyenge on a rowe
Bothe preest and clerke dyspoyled & all ouerthrowe
Sorowfull in her thought y^t she had taryed behynde
Amonge the tourmentes she dyde her selfe be knowe
So was she quelled in callynge cryste to her mynde

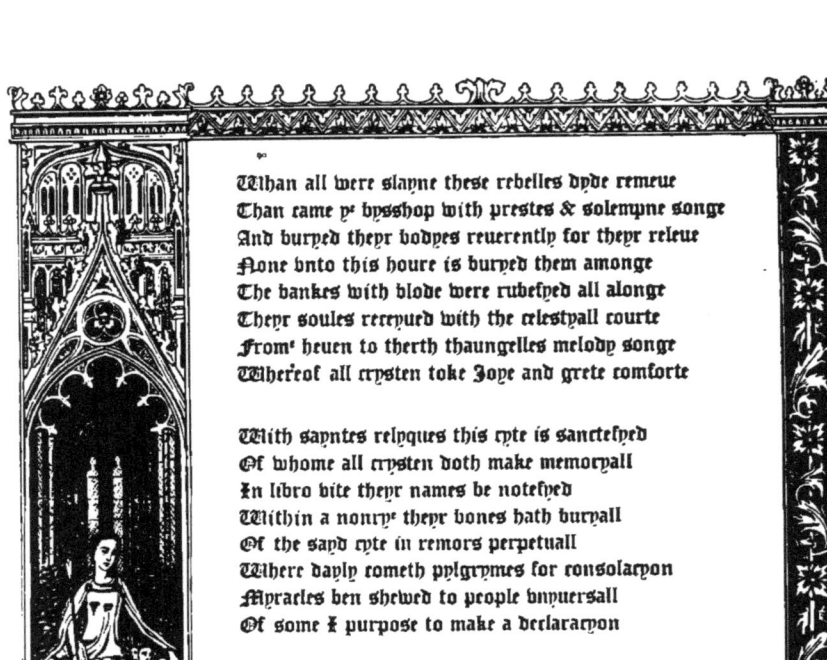

Whan all were slayne these rebelles dyde remeue
Than came ye bysshop with prestes & solempne songe
And buryed theyr bodyes reuerently for theyr releue
None vnto this houre is buryed them amonge
The bankes with blode were rubefyed all alonge
Theyr soules recyued with the celestyall courte
From heuen to therth thaungelles melody songe
Whereof all crysten toke Joye and grete comforte

With sayntes relyques this cyte is sanctefyed
Of whome all crysten doth make memoryall
In libro vite theyr names be notefyed
Within a nonrye theyr bones hath buryall
Of the sayd cyte in remors perpetuall
Where dayly cometh pylgrymes for consolacyon
Myracles ben shewed to people vnyuersall
Of some I purpose to make a declaracyon

An abbot there was not ferre frome Colen dwellynge
Herynge of the myracles desyred for consolacyon
To vysyte these virgyns deuocyon hym compellynge
Came to the nonrye to make his Immolacyon
Desyred of the abbesse for the virgyn laudacyon
One of theyr bodyes to reste in his abbaye
Promysynge ye abbesse with faythfull compnycacyon
Within a yere to sh rye her ornatlye

Cy est pourtraicte ma
dame Ste Ursule, et les
Unze Mille vierges:

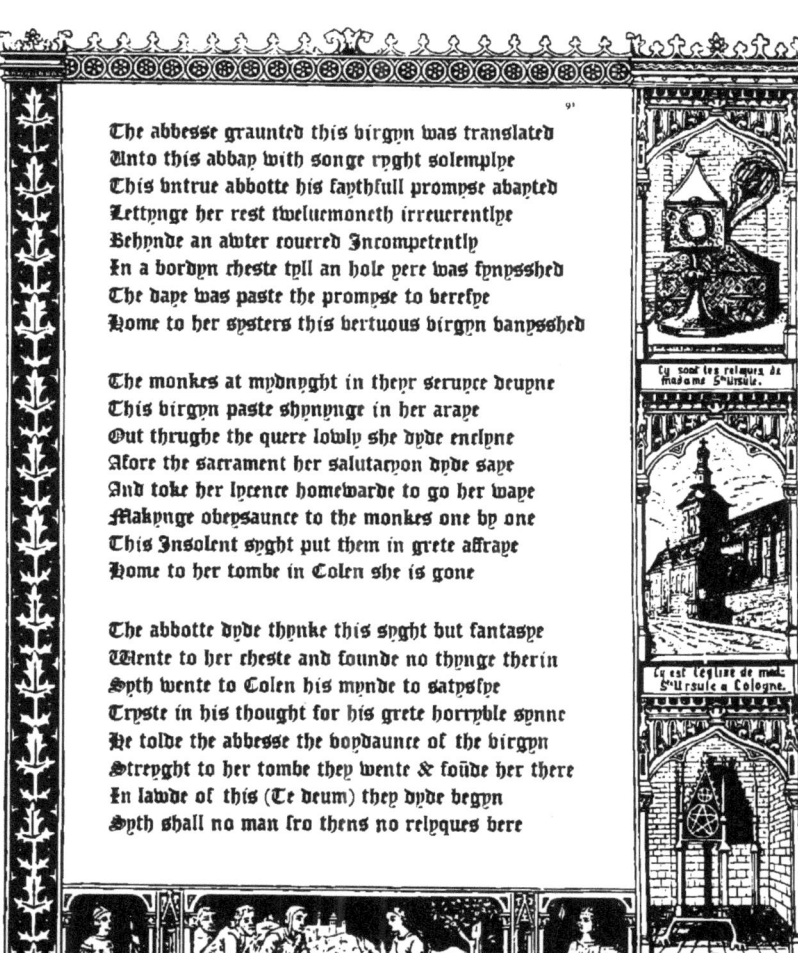

The abbesse graunted this birgyn was translated
Unto this abbay with songe ryght solemplye
This vntrue abbotte his faythfull promyse abapted
Lettynge her rest tweluemoneth irreuerentlye
Behynde an awter couered Incompetently
In a bordyn cheste tyll an hole yere was fynysshed
The daye was paste the promyse to verefye
Home to her systers this vertuous birgyn banysshed

The monkes at mydnyght in theyr seruyce deuyne
This birgyn paste shynynge in her araye
Out thrughe the quere lowly she dyde enclyne
Afore the sacrament her salutacyon dyde saye
And toke her lycence homewarde to go her waye
Makynge obeysaunce to the monkes one by one
This Insolent syght put them in grete affraye
Home to her tombe in Colen she is gone

The abbotte dyde thynke this syght but fantasye
Wente to her cheste and founde no thynge therin
Syth wente to Colen his mynde to satysfye
Cryste in his thought for his grete horryble synne
He tolde the abbesse the boydaunce of the birgyn
Streyght to her tombe they wente & foūde her there
In lawde of this (Te deum) they dyde begyn
Syth shall no man fro thens no relyques bere

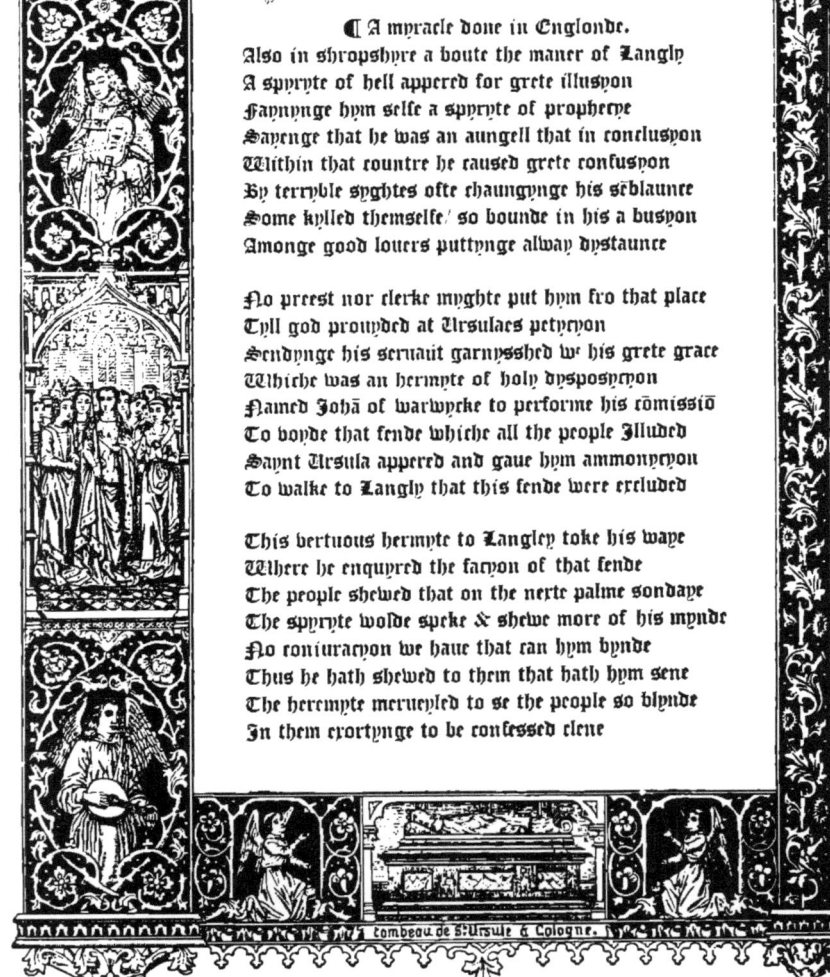

¶ A myracle done in Englonde.

Also in shropshyre a boute the maner of Langly
A spyryte of hell appered for grete illusyon
Faynynge hym selfe a spyryte of propherye
Sayenge that he was an aungell that in conclusyon
Within that countre he caused grete confusyon
By terryble syghtes ofte chaungynge his sēblaunce
Some kylled themselfe/ so bounde in his abusyon
Amonge good louers puttynge alway dystaunce

No preest nor clerke myghte put hym fro that place
Tyll god prouyded at Ursulaes petycyon
Sendynge his seruaut garnysshed wt his grete grace
Whiche was an hermyte of holy dysposycyon
Named Johā of warwycke to performe his cōmissiō
To voyde that fende whiche all the people Illuded
Saynt Ursula appered and gaue hym ammonycyon
To walke to Langly that this fende were excluded

This vertuous hermyte to Langley toke his waye
Where he enquyred the facyon of that fende
The people shewed that on the nexte palme sondaye
The spyryte wolde speke & shewe more of his mynde
No coniuracyon we haue that can hym bynde
Thus he hath shewed to them that hath hym sene
The hercmyte meruelyled to se the people so blynde
In them exortynge to be confessed clene

Tombeau de St Ursule à Cologne.

The day approched that this spyryte sholde appere
The people them kepte holy in contemplacyon
On palme sonday nyghte when all reposed were
It called the herempte by name of his appellacyon
Whiche answered/ and came at his vocacyon
Wenynge to hym it had ben the lorde of the place
He aspyed the spyryte whiche put hym in tribulacyō
His mynde dystracte to fle he had no space

Backwarde remenynge to the brynke of a water
The fende hym folowed in lykenes of a whele
All on a fyre the flambe abrode dyde shatter
To drowne the herempte this was his curst cautele
Whiche for the water myght flee hym neuer a dele
But suffred the fyre feruente with confydence
His clothes they brente his flesshe the fyre dyde fele
He called on cryst for payne in his defence

A voyce appered sayenge vnto that fende
Sathan seductour thy cause is clene cassate
The deuyl then answered here haue I lost my mynde
Now thou arte come my name is adnichylate
After that voyce the grete hete dyde abate
The voyce constraynynge the fende there too confesse
And shewe the cause wherfore he dyd awayte
To peruerte the people which shewed ye hole progresse

Thus sayd the spyryte here dwelled a synfull man
Whiche for two synnes was dampned perpetually
One for his rychesse whiche couetously he wan
And not dysposed where moost was necessary
A nother cause was he commytte culpably
To mary a woman his fayth he had promysed
Whiche afterwarde of his purpose dyde vary
Maryenge a nother faythles vnauysed

My purpose was the people to deceyue
Causynge this body so dampned to translate
Commaundynge straytly all other sayntes to leue
And it to worshyp as souerayne sanctifycate
Affermynge my selfe frome god annuncyate
Sayenge that it was the bones of a birgyn holy
And I the soule to make it ratyfycate
This was my purpose to cause ydolatrye

Also I caused the persone of rokysly
To drowne hym selfe with dyuerse many mo
Johñ darras esquyers to hange hym pryuely
And dyuers batayles ayenst the chyrche also
And all the people ydolatrye to do
Than the boyce caused the spyryte auoyde fro thens
Whiche sayd though I fro this habytacyon go
I haue moo felawes to kepe here resydens

Thus was the spyryte auoyded frome that place
The voyce with ye herempte had holy cōmunycacyon
Shewynge hym her name Ursula replete with grace
For whome our lorde had graunted grete consolacion
Unto all people that hath her in laudacyon
Frome sodayne deth frome fyre and all tempeste
From fallynge sykenes from enmye from dampnaciō
At her petycyon our lorde hath this conceste

Also yf a woman with chylde be trauaylynge
And call to Ursula for helpe in her affeccyon
Our lorde hathe graunted the chylde his crystenynge
And saue the woman at Ursulaes petycyon
This hathe she gyuen the herempte in commysspon
Unto all people this myracle to commende
With dyuers moo wherof is no dyssymcyon
Loke in her hystorye where more is comprehende

Also she charged the herempte that for her sake
His fapthfull dylygence in this he wolde emplye
And charge the byssop cōmaundement for to make
To all the curates to preche it solempnely
And her to reuerence with all her company
With certayne prayers wherof she hym instructe
To reuerence all her sypsters syngulerlye
The herempte promysed to be her true conducte

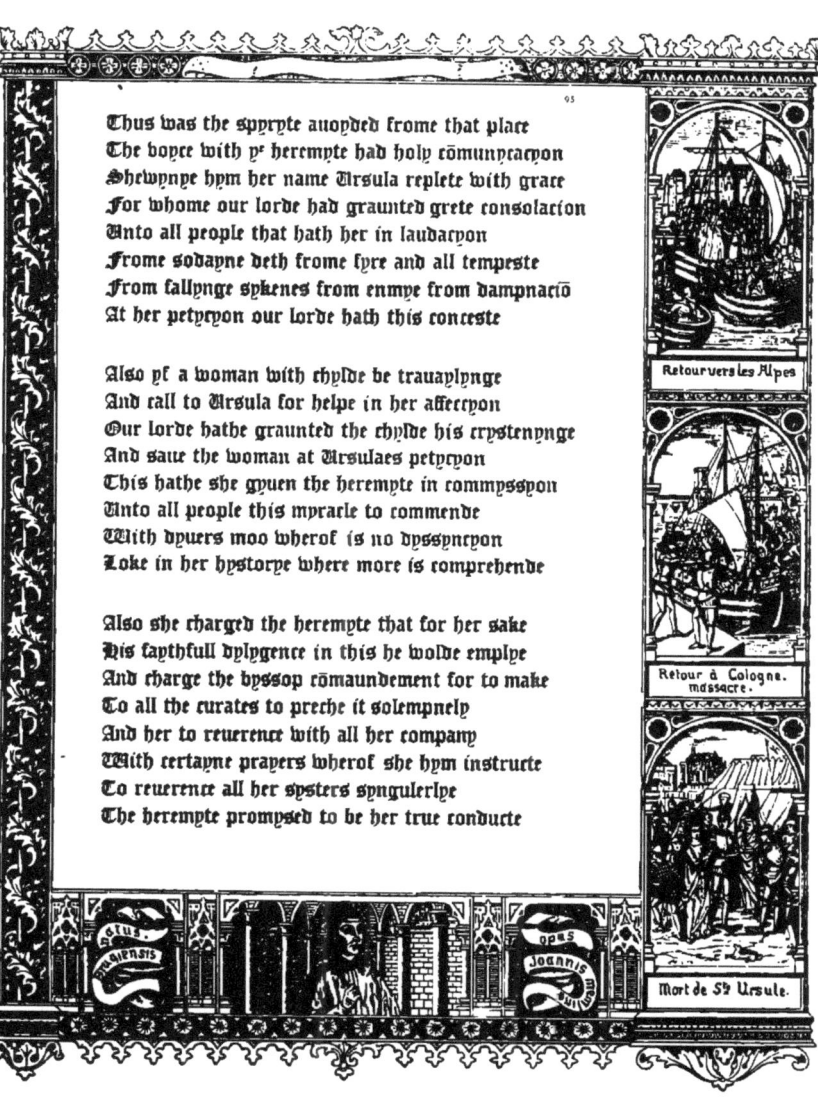

Retour vers les Alpes

Retour à Cologne.
massacre.

Mort de Ste Ursule.

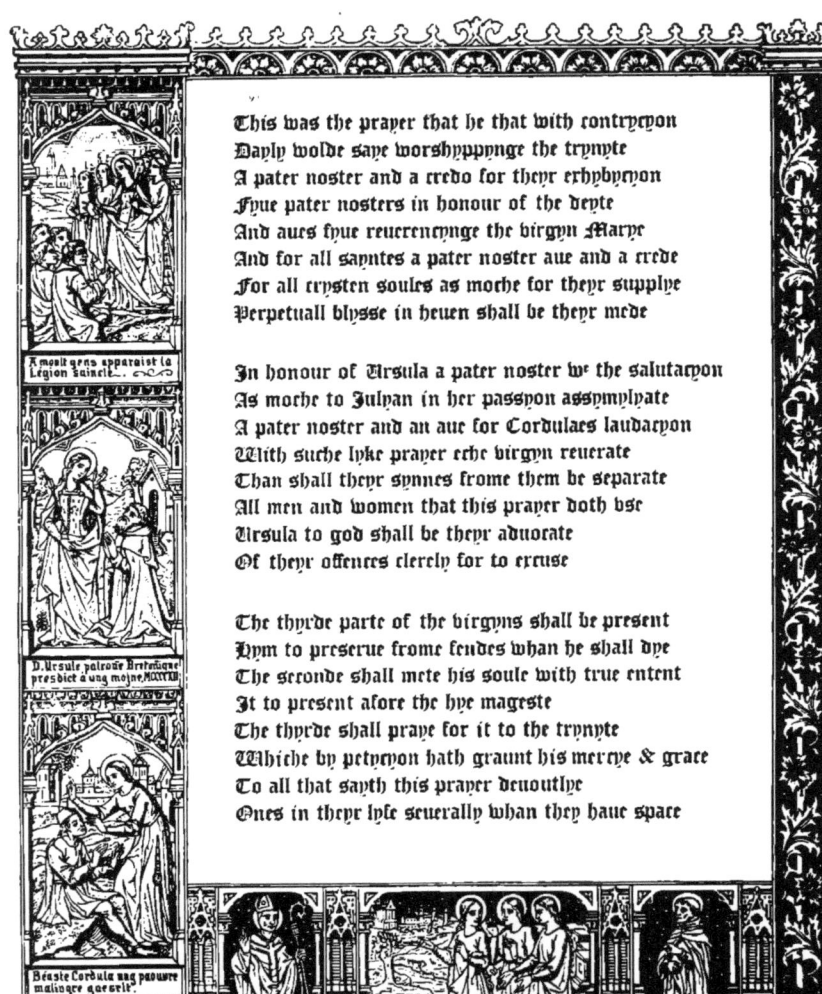

This was the prayer that he that with contrycyon
Dayly wolde saye worshyppynge the trynyte
A pater noster and a credo for theyr exhybycyon
Fyue pater nosters in honour of the deyte
And aues fyue reuerencynge the virgyn Marye
And for all sayntes a pater noster aue and a crede
For all crysten soules as moche for theyr supplye
Perpetuall blysse in heuen shall be theyr mede

In honour of Ursula a pater noster w^t the salutacyon
As moche to Julyan in her passyon assymplyate
A pater noster and an aue for Cordulaes laudacyon
With suche lyke prayer eche virgyn reuerate
Than shall theyr synnes frome them be separate
All men and women that this prayer doth vse
Ursula to god shall be theyr aduocate
Of theyr offences clerely for to excuse

The thyrde parte of the virgyns shall be present
Hym to preserue frome fendes whan he shall dye
The seconde shall mete his soule with true entent
It to present afore the hye mageste
The thyrde shall praye for it to the trynyte
Whiche by petycyon hath graunt his mercye & grace
To all that sayth this prayer deuoutlye
Ones in theyr lyfe seuerally whan they haue space

With this she banyshed the herempte in cōmaūdyng
That in her cause he wolde be dylygente
The herempte lauded our lorde and her knelynge
And shewed the people the vysyon and thentente
How the spyryte was gone at Ursulaes cōmaūdemēt
The people reioysed for voydaunce of the fende
Prayenge to the birgyns theyr souls to present
Unto that blysse enduryuge without ende

Who that these birgyns will serue with this prayer
Pater noster and aues he must saye .xi. dayly
Than shall they seuerally be serued in thre yere
Seruynge the fader and the sone with our lady
All sayntes all soules as I dyde patefye
Afore eche thousande and credes .xi. in order
Or elles eche daye pater nosters .xxx. and thre
Thus in one yere ye may them all honour

Thys myracle was shewed at Langely in shropshyre
The whiche grete nobylles by wrytynge do testefye
Of worthy men who lyst them to requyre
As abbottes and knyghtes & squyers of that countre
With syr Roberte lee lorde of the sayd Langly
To testefye the trouth theyr seales dyde appende
Which ben in Colen to shewe for a memorey
With many mo meruayles as sheweth her ture legede

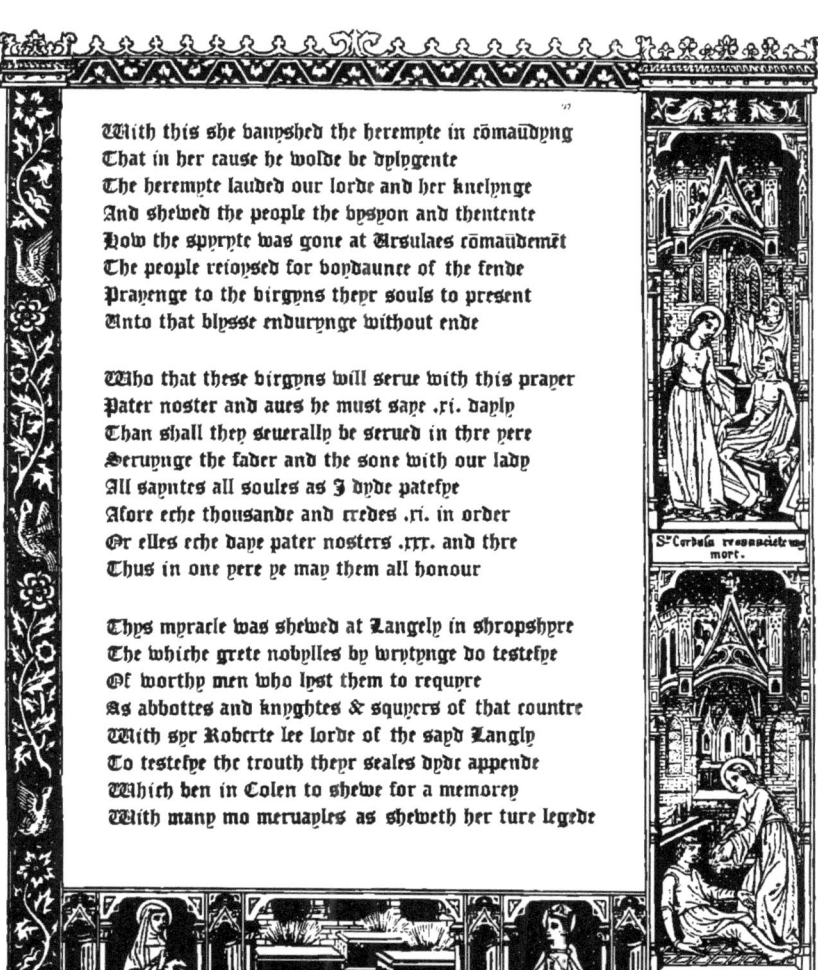

With soueraynte sayntes this cyte is sanctefyed
As with thre kynges to cryste that made oblacyon
Also wᵗ these virgȳs ryght mervaylously magnyfyed
Saynt Albon of englonde there resteth by traslacyon
With thousandes mo not knowen by nominacyon
In libro vite whose names ben comprehende
Now lette vs praye this turbe with contemplacyon
That all oure soules to cryst they may commende

℣ Vite sancte ursule sodaliumq. suarum
translata e sermone latino in anglicum /
rostratu fratris Edmūdi hatfeld monachi
Roffensis ac jussi illustrissime domine dñe
Margarete matris excellentissime princi
pis Henrici septimi. Impressa ūnit felice
ter per me Wynandum de worde Londo
niis cōmorantem in vico bulgarter dicto
the Fletestrete in signo solis et lune
℣ Sequitur oratio deuoto ad vndecim
milia birginum

℣ Oratio ad sanctum Ursulam et ad sodales suas
Concors chorus castitatis virginum et martirium
Ursula cum sociatis ad eternum bronium pro amore
trinitalis et regine virginum. vestris meritis adiuue

tiū et ope precaminū. bos colentes cum beatis secun-
dum bestrum meritum. bos in aduersis protegatis p
bestrum presidium. Et absolui faciatis al omni labe
Criminum. Ac post mortem perducatis ad eternum
gaudium .b. Orate pro nobis sponse dei electe. R. Ut
ad bestrū consorciū baleamus peruenire. Oremus
Omnipotēs sempiterne deus qui es sponsus bir
ginum premium martirum et pissimus exau-
ditor omnium sanctorū tuorum: meritis et precibus
gloriossimarum sponarū tuarū sanctissime Ursule
sociarumq. suarum birginū et martirum. concedere
digneris michi et omnibus eas benerantibus singu-
lorum peccatorum nostrorū beniam/ in adbersis ex-
pedientem protectionem/ in prosperis congruam direc
tionem et graciam nos confirmandi plenarie ad tuam
boluntatē michi sine illorum bisibilem consolationem
et cum illis transitum securum ad gloriam sempiter-
nam. Qui biris et regnas deus. per omnia secula secu
lorum. Amen.

arruez de la Flotte à Cologne

les XI.M. vierges à Basle.

D. Ursule et ses comp= à Rome.

Hospital S. Jean à Bruges.

APPENDIX.

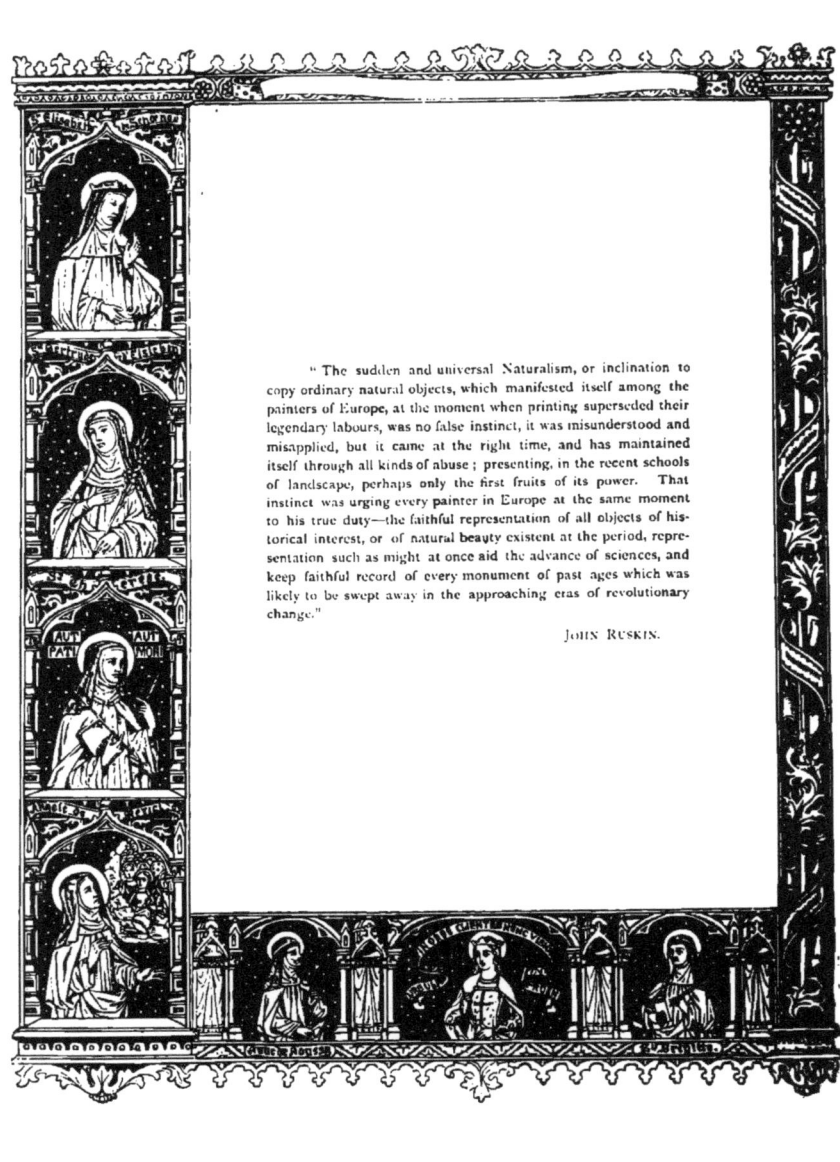

"The sudden and universal Naturalism, or inclination to copy ordinary natural objects, which manifested itself among the painters of Europe, at the moment when printing superseded their legendary labours, was no false instinct, it was misunderstood and misapplied, but it came at the right time, and has maintained itself through all kinds of abuse; presenting, in the recent schools of landscape, perhaps only the first fruits of its power. That instinct was urging every painter in Europe at the same moment to his true duty—the faithful representation of all objects of historical interest, or of natural beauty existent at the period, representation such as might at once aid the advance of sciences, and keep faithful record of every monument of past ages which was likely to be swept away in the approaching eras of revolutionary change."

JOHN RUSKIN.

HANS MEMLING:

AND

THE FLEMISH SCHOOL OF ART.

DURING the first centuries of the Christian era painting seems to have been but sparingly used in the decoration of churches. This probably arose from two causes; in the first place, the professors of the faith were so universally oppressed that but little opportunity was presented for such a purpose; and, in the second place, there still lingered amongst many of them certain Judaical notions, which prevented them from commemorating the principal events of the church's history by means of paintings, even if they had been at liberty to exercise the art unmolested. Nevertheless, we have very clear proof that

painting was practised at an early date amongst Christians, in the fact that the catacombs of Rome are profusely decorated with mural representations of saints, and occurrences recorded in the Holy Scriptures. As may be supposed, these works are extremely rude and inartistic; nevertheless they are the prototypes of a school of painting which subsequently obtained a most marvellous perfection.

When the seat of the Roman government was removed to Constantinople, that city for some centuries was regarded as the centre of the arts. Certain it is that the Byzantine artists exercised a great influence over the various schools of Western Europe, which may account in a great measure for the somewhat oriental display of gold and brilliant colours visible in early ecclesiastical pictures throughout Europe. From the middle of the twelfth and in the beginning of the thirteenth centuries visible signs appeared of a new life in art. It took a wider scope than heretofore; more artistic individuality was displayed; anatomical drawing was much improved, and expression more studied. Two centuries later a great revolution was wrought in painting. This was no less than the invention—or possibly, as some affirm, but the perfection—of

FLEMISH SCHOOL OF ART.

the system of working in oil, achieved by Hubert van Eyck, of Bruges, who, with his brother John, deserve to be regarded as the fathers of Flemish art. As may be supposed, in an age which produced more painters than any other, pupils were not wanting to learn the great secret of the van Eyck's: none amongst them achieved a higher reputation than Hans Memling—or as he is sometimes called Hemling. Born at Bruges about the year 1439, he entered the service of Charles the Bold, Duke of Burgundy, and being wounded in 1476 at the battles of Granson and Morat, he returned weary and destitute to his native town, and at the gates of the Hospital of St. John craved the succour he so much required. By the tender care of the monks of Saint John he was restored to health; and in some measure to repay them for their charity, he requested a place in the scriptorium to illuminate the missals and other devotional books produced by the scribes. It was while an inmate of this religious house that his marvellous genius developed itself, and those inimitable miniatures were executed which may be said to have almost immortalized him on earth.

At that time the relics of S. Ursula were preserved in an antique reliquary of rude workmanship, ornamented with a few

HANS MEMLING.

Dévostes Ursulines
resconfortées par
notre Dame.

pictures of a still ruder description. Memling—a devoted lover of the Church and its traditions—conceived the idea of constructing a more worthy receptacle for the hallowed contents. He communicated his design to Jan Floreins van der Rust, a brother holding some office in the hospital, and an ardent admirer of painting, who warmly applauded the pious intentions of Memling, and procured him the necessary materials to carry out the work. The result was the magnificent shrine now preserved at Bruges which has been the admiration of every succeeding age.

On entering the court-yard of the hospital, a small detached building on the left presents itself. It is there that the famous reliquary of S. Ursula is preserved. Carefully guarded for four centuries, the colours almost as brilliant as they appeared to the eyes of Memling himself, the world-renowned treasure seems to transport the spectator to ages long gone by. It requires but a feeble imagination to ascend the ever-flowing stream of time, and once more to live amongst the people of the fifteenth century; to breathe the same air, to feel the same sentiments, and to be imbued with the same living instincts as they. The manners, the costumes, the passions, the weaknesses,

FLEMISH SCHOOL OF ART.

the faith, depicted by the pencil of the artist, seem to be as unchangeable as nature herself. A subdued light illumines the pictures; a deep and almost religious silence reigns around; the distant lull of inarticulate murmurs from the busy city faintly strikes the ear, while before one—nay, in one's very grasp—lie the veritable, tangible remains of the mortal body of an immortal and sanctified spirit. *   *   *   *   *   *

The brothers van Eyck exhibit in their works more force than charm—the conception, the drawing, the colouring are distinguished by great firmness; but of the winsome power of poesy they seem to have been profoundly ignorant. Not so their pupil Memling, the Virgil of Flemish art; the ideal standard he set up for himself was far higher than that of the van Eycks: he attempted greater things than any of his predecessors, and he succeeded. But in his endeavours to depict glowing conceptions he did not neglect the essentials of his art. He studied anatomy carefully, and his drawing of the human figure far excels his masters. The hands and feet of his subjects are inimitable both in colour and form, and seem almost too delicate to belong to earth, and to be worthy rather of the holy messengers of God.

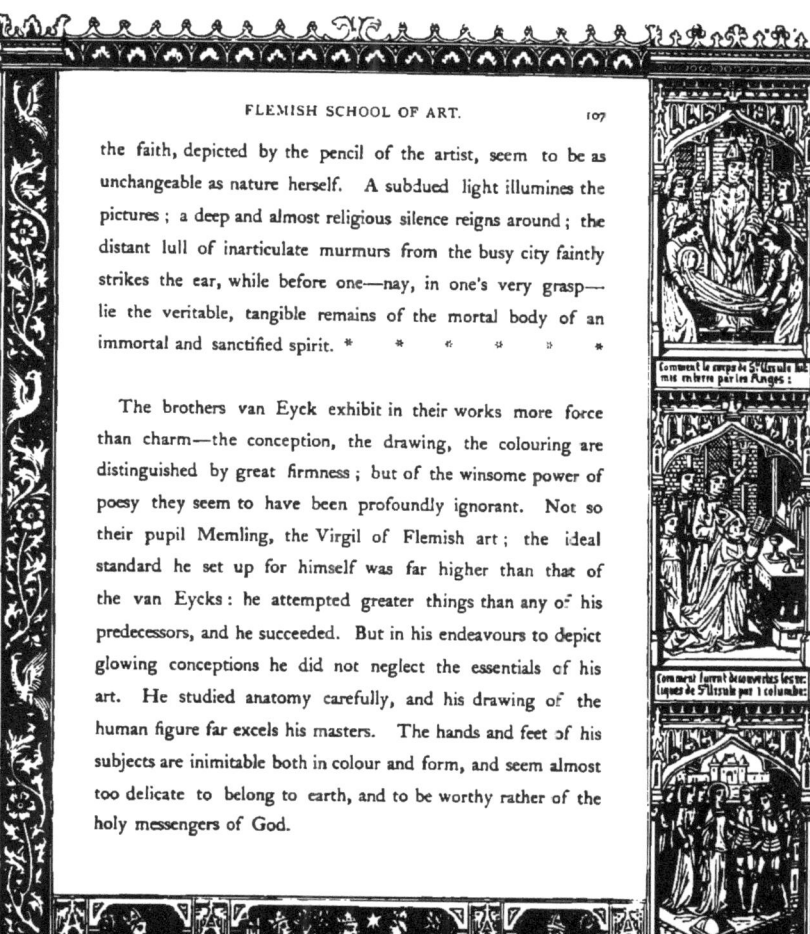

His draperies, less voluminous than those of the van Eycks, are more graceful, and seem to be worn by his subjects with much greater dignity. An overloading of accessories at all times indicates the decadence of art. The primitive artist restricts himself to his absolute necessities: a few trees, sparsely scattered, represent a forest; and a tiny rivulet is placed for a wide-spreading river. It is only at a later period, when art has reached the full devolopment of its maturity, that the artist learns to use rather than abuse the means at his disposal. The costumes of John van Eyck seem as though they were copied from the sculpture then in vogue. In both, the same inordinate fulness, the same conventional arrangements, the same profusion of folds are everywhere visible. Like architecture, painting had arrived at that state in which the accessories stifled the original: general forms were hidden under an efflorescence of bristling ornaments, and leading features of construction were lost amidst a profusion of details. The delicate appreciation of the requirements of art preserved Memling from being carried away by the follies of his contemporaries. Though occasionally we find him yielding in some degree to surrounding influences, he speedily returns to the true path—the

FLEMISH SCHOOL OF ART.

path marked out by the artists of Greece, and in which Raphael shortly afterwards followed.

The ideal enthusiasm which directed the pencil of Memling had not always the human figure for its object: he delighted, he almost revelled, in reproducing the fairest scenes of nature. The earth he mantles with the most velvety of turfs finished with such infinite care that when viewed through a magnifying glass—by the assistance of which the miniature must have been painted—the very blades of grass are plainly to be discerned: numberless flowers deck its smiling surface, and relieve its luxurious monotony. Here we see the wild strawberry with its delicate tendrils timidly exposing its spotless flowers and luscious fruit; the bright marsh mallow; the modest violet; and the flaring poppy. Beyond, the wild sage displays its curiously indented leaves; the St. John's wort opens its golden umbel; the homely centaury spreads its brilliant bloom, while around its stem creeps the elegant vetch, supporting itself delicately by its graceful tendrils. We love these flowers as ancient friends; with most of us they are associated with some pleasing recollections, and for their sake we respect the hand that traces them on the canvas.

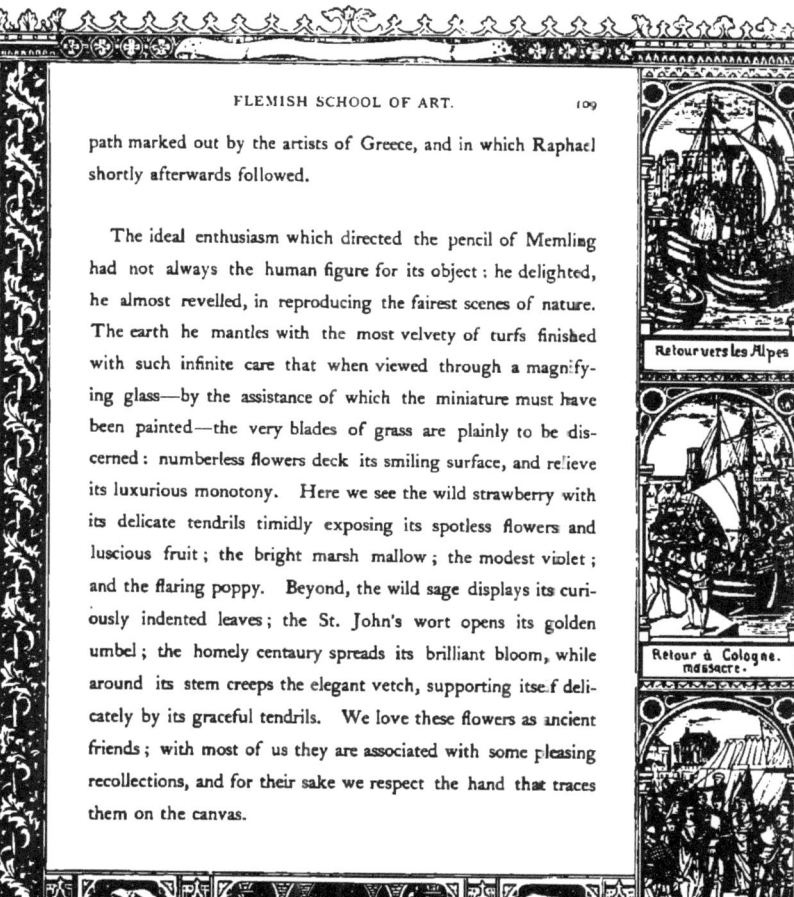

Retour vers les Alpes

Retour à Cologne. massacre.

Mort de Ste Ursule.

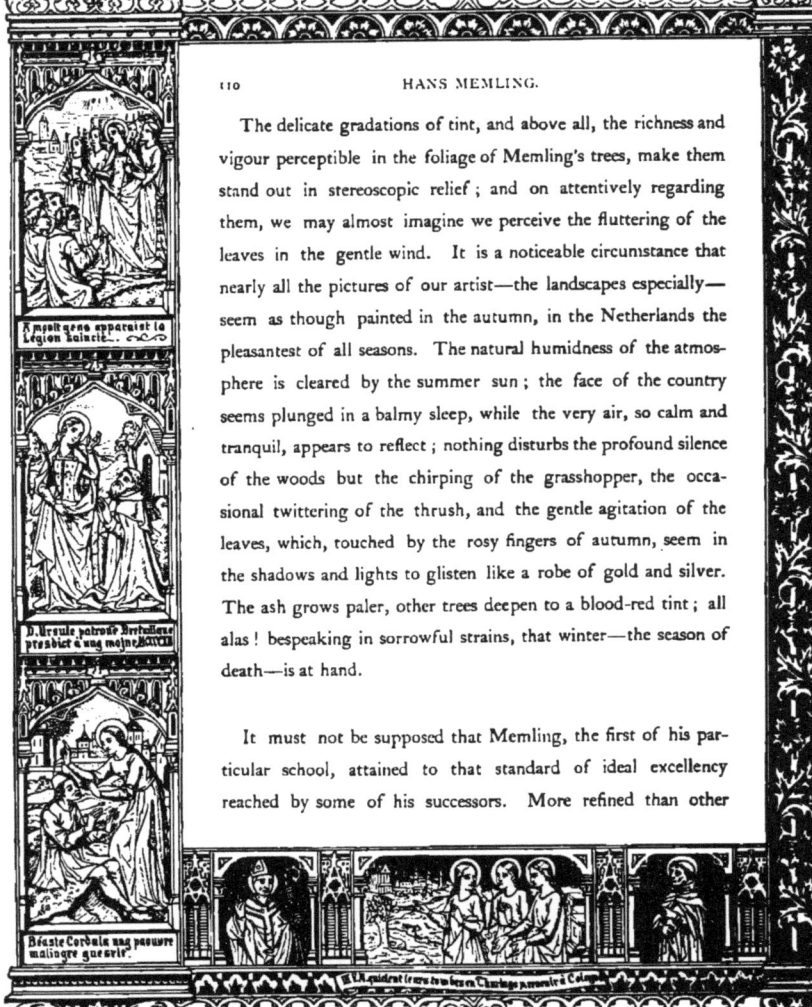

The delicate gradations of tint, and above all, the richness and vigour perceptible in the foliage of Memling's trees, make them stand out in stereoscopic relief; and on attentively regarding them, we may almost imagine we perceive the fluttering of the leaves in the gentle wind. It is a noticeable circumstance that nearly all the pictures of our artist—the landscapes especially— seem as though painted in the autumn, in the Netherlands the pleasantest of all seasons. The natural humidness of the atmosphere is cleared by the summer sun; the face of the country seems plunged in a balmy sleep, while the very air, so calm and tranquil, appears to reflect; nothing disturbs the profound silence of the woods but the chirping of the grasshopper, the occasional twittering of the thrush, and the gentle agitation of the leaves, which, touched by the rosy fingers of autumn, seem in the shadows and lights to glisten like a robe of gold and silver. The ash grows paler, other trees deepen to a blood-red tint; all alas! bespeaking in sorrowful strains, that winter—the season of death—is at hand.

It must not be supposed that Memling, the first of his particular school, attained to that standard of ideal excellency reached by some of his successors. More refined than other

FLEMISH SCHOOL OF ART.

Flemish artists, he is nevertheless grosser than those of the Italian school. A tinge of the coarseness of features of the Low Countries is perceptible in nearly all his faces; and one who expects to find in the works of Memling the æsthetic beauties of Masaccio, Perugino, or Raphael, will be disappointed. There is one strange peculiarity in many of his faces—the eyes do not converge to the same point; in other words, many of his characters are represented with a painful cast, in their sight. M. Michiels, an eminent art-critic, attempts to account for this peculiarity by supposing that Memling must have been similarly afflicted, on the principle that Poussin, whose eyes were constitutionally inflamed and totally destitute of lashes, painted all his subjects with a like deformity. So, too, Peter Aertsen, a Dutch painter of considerable merit, being himself remarkably tall, made all his men and women of colossal size, whereby he obtained the sobriquet of Peter the Long.

Memling seems to have imbibed the spirit of the age in his fondness for representing continuous stories, as in the series now under our particular notice. The painters and sculptors of the middle ages were not content to represent a single incident; they aimed at something higher, and considered no depicted narrative

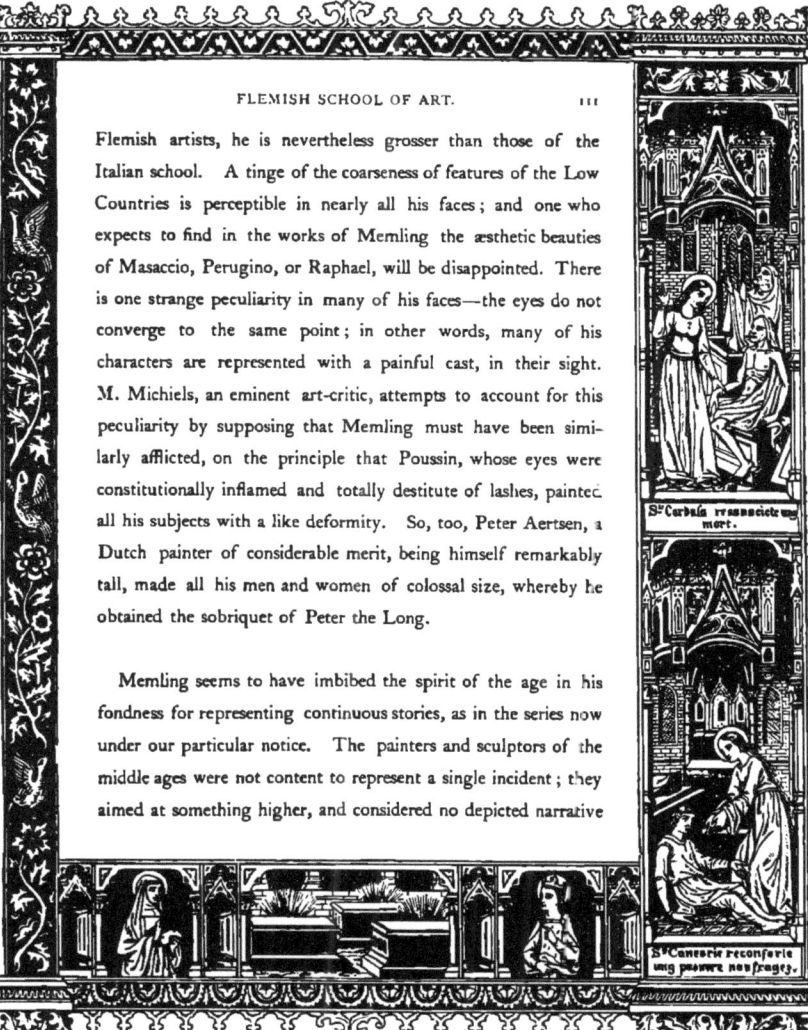

complete unless its every important circumstance was duly set forth. So too the modern drama, which took its rise about the same period, pursued a parallel course. The mysteries, as performed by the clerks, were frequently of enormous length, embracing episodes in the history of man from the time our first parents were placed in the garden of Eden down to the day of the last judgment. The representation of the *Mystery of the Passion*, which was extremely popular in France during the fifteenth century, extended over four days; and was contained in eighty-six acts and forty-one thousand verses. Another piece setting forth the life of Christ by means of a dialogue was commenced at Poictiers on the 19th of July, and was resumed daily until the 30th of the same month. The *Acts of the Apostles* occupied no less than forty days in its representation, and the number of actors engaged in it was almost incredible. The stage was an enormous structure, five or six stories in height, each story being divided into compartments; one representing the Temple; another the city of Damascus; another the Mediterranean sea, and so on throughout the entire history. Thus the drama undoubtedly exercised a great influence over the painters of the period, and led them to adorn altar-pieces, triptyches, missals, and other furniture of the church, with con-

FLEMISH SCHOOL OF ART.

nected incidents taken from the Bible, each episode within a separate compartment.

The shrine of S. Ursula, preserved at Bruges, is in the form of a small Gothic monument, with a pointed roof and buttresses. A statuette is placed at each corner representing S. Agnes, S. Helen, S. John the Evangelist, and S. James. S. Ursula, sheltering her companions under her mantle, is painted on one end under a canopy of Gothic tracery, the Blessed Virgin occupies the other, holding on her right arm the infant Jesus, to whom she is offering an apple. Between the columns on either side are represented the various incidents connected with the pilgrimage of S. Ursula. They are six in number: the first is a drawing of Cologne—probably as seen by Memling; certainly not as it existed in the time of S. Ursula. Sigillindis is standing on the quay, and welcomes the British virgin as she debarks from her vessel. In the middle distance is a spacious mansion, through one of the windows of which we see S. Ursula on her couch, receiving the inspired message, and, in an adjoining apartment Florentina apparently engaged in prayer.

The second miniature represents the arrival of the holy com-

pany of martyrs at Bâle. Two vessels occupy the foreground: S. Ursula, distinguished by her robe of ermine, has just landed; while far in the distance we see a long train of the virgins who are making their way by a devious path towards the snow-covered Alps, which seem to present an unsurmountable barrier to their progress.

The third picture shews us the Pope Cyriacus receiving the holy pilgrims. This is certainly one of the most beautiful of the charming series: if there be any fault in its composition it is that the number of spectators who would naturally be drawn together to witness such an extraordinary event as the arrival of so many foreign visitors, is far too small. This, perhaps, is but a minor objection amply atoned for by the incomparable beauty of the picture itself. In the foreground is the holy pope fully habited in his pontifical vestments. He is represented as standing just without the doors of a church, and in his attitude and expression seems the ideal of majesty and benevolence. S. Ursula humbly kneels before him: from under a fillet which encircles her head, her lustrous fair hair ripples down in a golden stream. No artist ever excelled Memling in the manner in which he represents the ravishing beauty of long flowing hair;

Tombeau de St Ursule à Cologne.

FLEMISH SCHOOL OF ART.

the effect produced by a few touches of his masterly hand is indescribably beautiful. The Pope seems in the attitude of raising S. Ursula; he holds both her hands in his left, while, with his right uplifted, he is giving his benediction. A long procession of pilgrims approaches from the distance, among them appear several habited differently to those in the former paintings. These are probably virgins who have joined the company during their progress from Cologne. At the right hand of the picture are neophytes receiving the sacrament of baptism by immersion; and in the background S. Ursula herself appears communicating in the temple.

On the other side of the shrine, which, it may be mentioned revolves on a pivot for the purpose of being more easily examined, we see the company embarking at Bâle for Cologne. Cyriacus, the Pope, it will be remembered, received a divine intimation to return with the holy pilgrims. He is represented sitting in the stern of the principal vessel with two cardinals at his side, giving his benediction to the fleet before its departure. S. Ursula is in the fore-part of the boat, standing between Celindris and Florentina, with hands clasped and eyes upraised as though engaged in silent prayer. In another part of the same

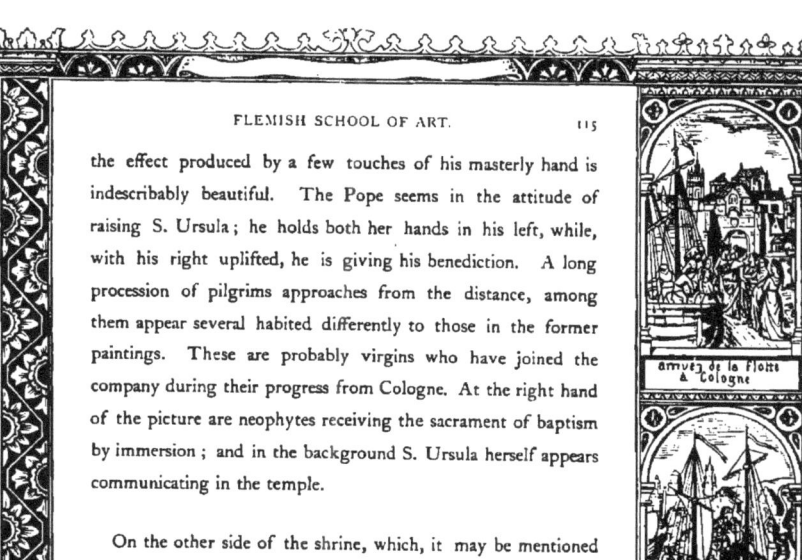

picture the band of martyrs is seen approaching the port of embarkation.

The fifth and sixth pictures represent the massacre of the blessed virgins. In the former two archers are shooting their arrows at the martyrs. One of the virgins buries her face in her hands; another, pierced through the arm by an arrow, stands erect awaiting her end with heroic courage. A number of armed soldiers rush upon the defenceless maidens, many of whom are seen lying prostrate on the ground, covered with horrible wounds. S. Ursula holds the bleeding body of one of her followers in her arms, and is vainly attempting to shield her from the fury of a barbarian armed with a sword. In the sixth picture the horrid carnage is continued. It would be difficult to praise this admirable work of art too highly; the attitudes of the figures, and the various expressions of the faces are every way worthy of the great painter. S. Ursula, standing erect, calmly awaiting the arrow which an archer is fitting to his bow, is in herself a picture. Action is displayed throughout the whole composition; every one seems to move; and, looking at the fearful scene, the spectator can almost imagine he hears the hoarse shout of the barbarous Huns, " Death to the Christians," mingled with the sighs and groans of the dying virgins.

FLEMISH SCHOOL OF ART.

Upon the roof of the precious reliquary is depicted the glorification of S. Ursula in the presence of the holy Trinity. Angels are singing and making melody on their harps, and below, the vicar of Christ prostrates himself while the virgin saint receives the blessed crown of her martyrdom.

In the year 1794, Belgium nearly lost her greatest treasure. The French commissioners presented themselves at the Hospital of St. John; and, in ignorance of the local name, demanded *La châsse.* The brothers not readily understanding the exact nature of the demand, assured the Commission they only held custody over *La ryve* de Saint Ursule, and the Frenchmen, not being aware that the two names were really identical in meaning, went in quest of other spoils. Thus France, through the want of a little local knowledge on the part of her emissaries, failed to possess this sacred reliquary.

The magnificent series of miniatures, which illustrate the present work, is preserved in the church of S. Ursula at Cologne. Each miniature is enclosed in a small frame, and at the bottom is inscribed in antique German characters an explanatory verse. It is only recently that these verses have been discovered: for many years they had been concealed

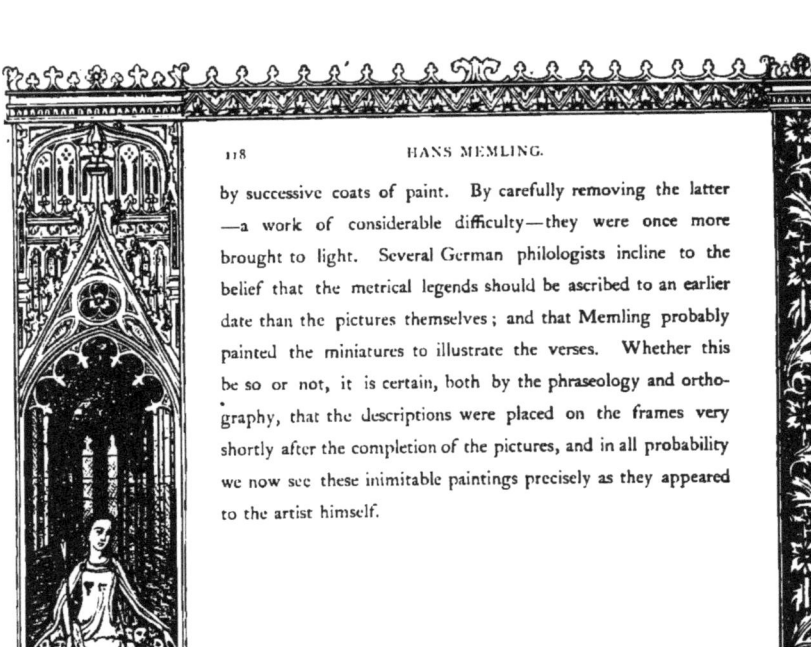

by successive coats of paint. By carefully removing the latter —a work of considerable difficulty—they were once more brought to light. Several German philologists incline to the belief that the metrical legends should be ascribed to an earlier date than the pictures themselves; and that Memling probably painted the miniatures to illustrate the verses. Whether this be so or not, it is certain, both by the phraseology and orthography, that the descriptions were placed on the frames very shortly after the completion of the pictures, and in all probability we now see these inimitable paintings precisely as they appeared to the artist himself.

ROMAN INSCRIPTION.

ONE of the most interesting records of Saint Ursula and her companions which remains to us is the Roman slab on a wall in the choir of the church which bears her name at Cologne. As the transcript on the last page may not be intelligible to some of our readers, we subjoin a translation of this curious inscription :—

"*The Consul Clematius frequently incited by divine visions and attracted by the renown of the martyrdom of the heavenly virgins, came from the East, and in fulfilment of a vow, restored this church from its foundations at his own cost. Should any one deposit in this church—where the holy virgins poured out their blood for Christ—any body except that of a virgin, may he know that he will be punished with flames of everlasting fire.*"

Not far from this interesting slab is raised a monument, or what is now commonly termed an altar-tomb, bearing an inscription, from which we learn it was erected to Viventia, whom tradition informs us was the daughter of Pepin

ROMAN INSCRIPTION.

d'Heristal. On one end is the date of erection—644; and on one of its sides an inscription in Roman capitals to this effect:—

Clematius, in restoring this temple in the year 426, forbade any body to be here interred.

On the other side we read:—

Viventia twice buried here, and as often rejected by the earth, at length finds a resting place within this mausoleum.

We are not informed in what manner the earth twice rejected the body of Viventia; but that the fact was as recorded there can be but little doubt, for the tomb which commemorates the circumstance was erected at the time of its occurrence, when every one must have been perfectly familiar with it, and any misstatement would have been immediately discovered and exposed.